Tony Kirwood is a writer, teacher and a broadcast on TV and radio in Britain an produced sketch shows on the London he has been teaching comedy writing and su colleges, writers' weekends and at his own independent venue writing students have gone on to success, selling material to the BBC, producing radio shows and winning competitions. His standup comedy students have reached the finals of national and London-wide competitions. He also writes humorous articles and blogs.

Also available from HowTo Books

HOW TO WRITE COMEDY

**Discover the building blocks of sketches, jokes
and sitcoms – and make them work**

Tony Kirwood

Constable & Robinson Ltd
55–56 Russell Square
London WC1B 4HP
www.constablerobinson.com

First published in the UK by How to Books,
an imprint of Constable & Robinson, 2014

A copy of the British Library Cataloguing in Publication Data
is available from the British Library

ISBN: 978-1-84528-525-8 (paperback)
ISBN: 978-1-84528-561-6 (ebook)

1 3 5 7 9 10 8 6 4 2

Printed and bound in the EU

CONTENTS

LIST OF ILLUSTRATIONS

PREFACE

COMEDY IS IN DEMAND

The first recorded joke was written down in Ancient Sumeria in about 1800 BC. It went something like this:

'Something which has not occurred since time immemorial: that a young woman did not fart till her husband's embrace.'

You can bet that the writer sat back with a satisfied smirk, hopefully holding a cheque (or chunk of scratched wax) for the going rate. You can also bet that hundreds of aspiring comedy writers were muttering, 'I can do better than that', into their beer.

The style and subject matter of comedy may have changed (although fart jokes have clearly been around for a while), but society has always recognized the importance of laughter and rewarded those who can create it. A successful comedy writer can make a good living. A very successful one can live in style.

Scanning my *Radio Times* this week I counted eleven episodes of new sitcoms on TV and ten on radio, five new sketch and broken comedy shows on TV, five on radio, and ten TV game and presented shows which use comedy material. This doesn't include the classic repeats on terrestrial, digital and cable channels, which probably run into hundreds of episodes.

And I haven't counted the hundreds of thousands of comedy videos and clips jostling for space on the internet. Comedy continues to be a vital part of our lives.

Will awakens enthusiasm.

The I Ching

UNDERSTANDING THE CHALLENGES

COMEDY CAN BE HARD TO WRITE

It can seem a hard nut to crack when you're starting out. Good ideas can be dispiritingly elusive. You can stare at your screen a whole morning with nothing coming into your head. And even when an idea does hit you, it can be hard to shape it into a sketch or sitcom that works. The writing doesn't seem funny enough. It doesn't do justice to the idea. You may spend weeks on a script which you started in a fit of inspiration, to find that the characters seem thin or the concept threadbare.

COMEDY CAN BE HARD TO SELL

Even when you've written something of which you feel proud, finding an outlet for it can be difficult. At times you may feel that the comedy industry is run by insiders who are set on blocking the entry of bright newcomers like yourself. You're warned that a sitcom by an unknown writer has a tiny chance of being commissioned. You find that comedians write their own jokes or use a tight group of people they've known for years. TV and radio comedy output seems to be written by an inner circle who have closed their ranks. To rub salt into your wounds, you know that you have written material that is just as good as some of that which is produced. You have as much talent as those writers. How come they are in and you are out?

GRASPING THE OPPORTUNITIES

Stop there. Look at it in a different light. Now is a great time to be a comedy writer. Comedy is changing rather than shrinking. Some routes to success may have closed, but others are opening up. Technology has made possible a new range of opportunities and people's need to laugh is as strong as ever.

THE BBC

Our biggest broadcaster has a remit to encourage new talent. They continue to produce programmes specifically designed to showcase new writers. Without a flow of fresh people coming through the doors of Broadcasting House, comedy would become stale and safe. BBC Radio, in particular, is open to new ideas and faces.

COMMERCIAL BROADCASTERS

Although they don't have the same public service ethos, Channel 4 and the other commercial companies are always on the lookout for funny writers with a fresh angle. The route through their doors may be less direct than the BBC, but they know they won't produce another *Father Ted* without keeping an eye on emerging talent.

THE INTERNET

- *Videos.* Although having a script accepted by a major TV or radio channel remains the best way to success and payment, nowadays for the price of a camera you can reach a potentially large audience on sites such as YouTube. In between sending off your material to broadcasters, you can produce your own sketches, animations and quirky videos. They won't make you rich, but you can get your work noticed.
- *Competitions.* The prizes may vary from thousands of pounds and working with BBC producers to a showing on a website with your name below. Either way, your work will be getting out there and your reputation can spread.

THE LIVE STAGE

The rage for comedy clubs shows no sign of abating. If you have the urge to perform your jokes as a standup comedian or join a group of sketch performers, you greatly increase your chance of being noticed. If this is too far out of your comfort zone, try getting involved with a sketch team as a writer. *Little Britain* and *The League of Gentlemen* had their origins on the standup stage.

Nonsense wakes up the brain cells. And it helps develop a sense of humour, which is awfully important in this day and age. Humour has a tremendous place in this sordid world. It's more than just a matter of laughing. If you can see things out of whack, then you can see how things can be in whack.

Dr Seuss

COMEDY WRITING IS A CRAFT

It's one thing to know that there are outlets for your talent, it's another to be able to come up with a flow of funny material. You may have what seems like a good idea, but to convert it into a concrete piece of comedy can seem like chiselling smoke. Treat the process as if you were making a table. First you must lay your hands on the raw material, which in comedy is the life all around us, and then use techniques to turn it into a usable shape. Your writing is a skill which only improves with constant practice.

Most successful comedy writers will tell you they didn't become funny overnight. They learnt to write good scripts through a hard process of trial, submissions, rejections, rewrites and graft.

GETTING IDEAS

Much of this book deals with a comedy writer's first task: to find ideas. They're not always easy to come by, but practice and getting into the mindset will help you overcome blocks. It may sound counter-intuitive, but getting in touch with your inspiration is a skill like any other.

ADOPTING A STRUCTURED APPROACH

Writing is best done systematically. Moving steadily through the stages of finding an idea, creating a structure, writing and honing the dialogue and progressive rewrites takes much of the anxiety out of writing sketches, jokes and sitcoms. It may seem rather a 'doing it by numbers' approach, but following the process closely will allow your creative instinct to flourish.

UNDERSTANDING EACH GENRE

Many of the 'rules' of comedy are constant throughout all its formats. But, from the point of view of the writer, each genre demands a different discipline and mindset. The comedy genres are:

- Sketches
- Jokes
- Sitcoms
- Stage plays
- Feature films
- Novels

In this book we'll be looking in depth at the first three. Novels take a narrative rather than dramatic form: the events are usually in the past rather than acted out before our eyes and are described in continuous prose. Film screenplays and stage plays are highly complex with distinct structures and ways of working. The industries for these genres work in a different way from those of broadcast and live comedy.

This leaves sketches, jokes and sitcoms, the most common everyday forms. Most developing writers tackle them in that order, which is the sequence in this book. All the genres have many things in common, but they all make very different demands on the writer. For example, when you set out on your first sitcom, you'll find that the techniques you picked up writing sketches and jokes will be a big help but also that you will need a fresh approach to meet a very different challenge.

HOW TO USE THIS BOOK

I recommend that you follow the chapters in sequence. The skills you learn are progressive and often transferable from one genre to the next. If you have an idea for a sitcom, the chapters on writing sketches will give you confidence in storytelling and character, which are central to sitcoms.

If, however, your idea is burning a hole in your head and you can't wait, then by all means head for the sitcom section first. But go back to the earlier chapters as soon as you can.

This is a manual, not a theoretical guide. The emphasis is often on technique and method rather than inspiration. That's because inspiration comes quicker when you know what you're doing. By following the exercises you will start up what will become a portfolio of sketches, jokes and a sitcom which you can begin to submit to producers, or even perform or produce yourself.

BEING A WRITER

From now on, you're a professional writer. Even if you haven't yet sold or even sent off a script, take your work seriously. Start to jot down your ideas, however vague, to look for markets, to study both contemporary and classic comedy, and to work out how you can find your place in it.

Above all, start to open up your mind. You're on the first step of discovery of the myriad, crazy, critical and celebratory ways by which comedy brightens the way we live. It's a life-affirming journey. You'll learn how to look at the world in new ways and, best of all, to express your vision to other people and make them laugh. You'll stay constant to the way you see things, but be better able to communicate it to others. Comedy is a way of getting people to see an unexpected truth that you will light for them.

See this book as a key to open up what's already inside you. So – you supply the talent. You have a sense of your inner creative map and what wonderful episodes of comic craziness you're capable of making. I don't. But I can help you realize it. So let's get on with the job.

Exercise

Think of three TV or radio comedy shows you know – two you like and one you don't like. Ask yourself of the two you like, 'Why are they funny?' and write down the answers. Ask of the third one, 'Why don't I find it funny?' And then, 'Why was it considered funny enough to be commissioned?'

1
WRITING SKETCHES: AN INTRODUCTION

WHY WRITE SKETCHES?

There's nothing more creative and fun than writing sketches. You can paint scenes as surreal as Salvador Dalí or an observational miniature on an aspect of daily life. You can create characters as mad as any of those in a comic. You can put aside a premise and pick up another like a prospector fingering nuggets.

THE BUILDING BLOCKS OF COMEDY

If comedy is a drama that makes us laugh, sketches are where it all begins. You must find a comic idea, people it with funny characters, set them in conflict and then resolve it, all in the space of two minutes. You'll have done what sitcom or movie writers do, but in a nutshell.

A GREAT TRAINING GROUND

It follows that sketch-writing skills will equip you brilliantly for all forms of writing. You'll learn how to come up with a constant flow of funny ideas. You'll write characters, dialogue and jokes. You'll create dramatic situations. Best of all, you'll learn the art of brevity. Distilling and refining your ideas into a two-minute format are important transferable skills which will make your sitcoms, screenplays and novels sharper and tighter. And they'll really help you get to grips with jokes and one-liners.

Many successful comedy writers got their first breaks by writing sketches. Today there are regular BBC sketch shows (usually on radio) for new writers. Sketch comedy is vibrant on the standup circuit. And, within its limitations, YouTube is a good showcase for sketches.

SKETCHES ARE SHORT

This doesn't mean you write them without effort. After a bit of practice, however, you'll be able to create and hone a workable sketch in a few hours. Compare this with the months needed to write a sitcom or the two years you have to spend on a screenplay and you'll see why it's a good idea to begin on the nursery slopes of sketches.

Feeling enthused? Let's begin at the beginning.

WHAT IS A SKETCH?

First of all, a sketch is:

- *A story.* A situation is unfolding. Events build and, in one way or other, are resolved. Even the most apparently static sketch has a developing storyline to keep the viewer or listener hooked.
- *Short.* The typical length these days is two minutes or even one. Up to about fifteen years ago, TV sketches could be five or six minutes. Then along came *The Fast Show*, with its thirty-second vignettes, and the comedy world changed. These days you need to think short.
- *Dramatic.* Things happen 'before our eyes' as opposed to narrated events from the past (which is what you usually find in a novel). You're writing dialogue and action.
- *Funny.* Well, of course. Maybe I needn't have said that. But I did anyway.

On top of this, sketches usually:

- *Use one location.* It's cheaper, simpler and faster. You may see sketches on TV which move from place to place but you're advised to stick to the one set. This is a good discipline to practise right from the start.
- *Use a limited cast.* Three or four characters are comfortable. With five, your house is becoming crowded. Can your four-person idea become a three? Or your three-character piece, a two? Brutally shoot your unneeded soldiers.

- *Contain conflict.* A good sketch will have a level of jeopardy, a bone of contention between the characters. It doesn't have to be violent or extreme.
- *Show one action in real time.* A single event is enacted in the same time it would have taken to happen. Two minutes of action mean a two-minute sketch. This means that things can build quicker, the flow isn't interrupted and, importantly, it's cheaper. And, at the risk of seeming to harp on, it's a great discipline.

Creativity is that marvellous capacity to grasp mutually distinct realities and draw a spark from their juxtaposition.

Max Ernst

UNDERSTANDING THE SKETCH GENRES

There are as many kinds of sketch as there are sketches. However, there are two overall genres which involve quite different writing approaches. They are:

THE IDEA SKETCH

This is what we'll be looking at in the next few chapters. It's based on a unique, distinctive premise. For example, four Indians go for a meal in an English restaurant in Bombay and behave as badly as English people do when they go 'for an Indian'. That sketch, 'Going for an English', helped make *Goodness Gracious Me* a massive success.

Or it could be a caped superhero whose superpower is the ability to mend bicycles (Monty Python's 'Bicycle Repair Man'). These are both one-off pieces, the classic type of modern sketch. We need to distinguish them from:

THE CHARACTER SKETCH

This relies entirely on its characters for the comedy. They return time and time again for us to laugh at their antics and the way they talk. Unlike idea sketches, these sketches always run in a series, for as long as the writers and performers can get laughs out of the character. We'll look at this genre later on.

> ### Exercise
> Make a list of five TV or radio sketch shows you know. For each of them, ask yourself if the comedy depends on stand-alone sketches or on running characters. If there's a mixture, what is the proportion?

WHAT MAKES US LAUGH?

There are nearly as many theories about this as there are jokes. You can approach the question from a sociological viewpoint, a historical one, a critical one or a creative one and come out with a different answer every time.

RELIEF

One theory is that laughter is an expression of relief. It goes something like this: an early human saw a sabretooth tiger and was ready to run when he realized it was a donkey. The sudden evaporation of intense fear caused a laugh. It makes psychological sense, though the incident is rather hard to prove.

THE UNEXPECTED

This theory is similar to the first, but without the element of relief. For example, a conductor in formal evening dress turns to face the orchestra, raises his baton – and his trousers fall down. We may not feel relief at the sight, but laugh because it came completely out of the blue.

BREAKING THE RULES

You could also say that the trouserless conductor is funny because a formal convention is subverted. In an instant, we move from a respectful situation to a rude one. From this perspective, comedy is essentially anarchic. The established order is broken: the toff becomes a tramp.

CRUELTY

We laugh because we feel superior to the conductor. The fully dressed people in the audience take pleasure from deriding the one person who isn't. The joke has a clear victim and the closed group torments the outsider with laughter. So, far from being subversive, comedy is conservative or even reactionary.

INAPPROPRIATE JUXTAPOSITION

If we had seen the conductor getting ready to get into a bath or go to bed, then there would be nothing funny about dropping his trousers. What was right for one situation becomes hilarious when placed in another. But if he was about to get into the bath and put on a top hat, we'd laugh.

STARTING TO FIND IDEAS FOR SKETCHES

But we're not here as social theorists. We have a practical purpose: we want to create the laughs, not analyse them. When you're writing an idea sketch you need a funny premise to sustain its momentum. Once you've found one that works, you're halfway there. So all you have to do is stumble across a great idea, write it out and wham bam! you have a great sketch. Sounds simple, doesn't it?

Well – it can be. Once in a blue moon. Sometimes a bolt of inspiration *does* strike a happy writer. Most of the time, however, the heavens simply don't open. To find comedy gold we have to dig. And sometimes we have to dig quite a lot to find a single nugget. The good news is that there are a lot of techniques we can use to make the digging less back-breaking.

COLLIDING WORLDS

- *Inappropriate juxtaposition*: you can create comedy by getting two or more realities to clash. Separately they may be completely unfunny but together they are absurd and inappropriate. Think of the top-hatted man stepping into the bath. Graham Linehan and Arthur Mathews followed up their huge *Father Ted* hit with the sketch show *Big Train*. Much of its surreal humour came from the juxtaposition of contrasting realities. In one sketch, the singer Chaka Khan shoots it out in a bloody Wild West gun battle with the Bee Gees. Another sketch took the form of a mock social documentary about farmers at a bidding auction, not for cattle, but for a trailerload of 1980s New Romantics. Pop singers in the Wild West. Fey 1980s trendies in a dirty cattle truck. You can see the comedy possibilities.

- *Juxtaposition of elements from the same world*: look at an aspect of modern life, for example shopping. Imagine a couple of young hoodies looking at the kit in a high-street sports-gear shop. It's a normal enough scenario. But in this shop the assistants have the mannerisms of top-end Savile Row tailors. How would the hoodies react? How would the shop assistants behave?

- *Juxtaposition of completely different worlds*: our hoodies go into another sports-gear shop but all this one has on sale is haddock. Again, how would they react? How would the shop assistant try to persuade them that haddock is just what a streetwise kid needs?

Exercise
Look at five sketches from two or three well-known shows. Are any of them based on colliding worlds? What are the realities that are clashing?

→ NOW TRY THIS

Think of a mundane element of your everyday life, for example, getting on to a train. With what could you juxtapose to it to create absurdity? For example, how would the train passengers behave if another mode of transport showed up, say an elephant or a space shuttle?

The easiest thing to do on earth is not write.

William Goldman, screenwriter

Exercise

Think of an aspect of contemporary life (for example, dating or smartphones). Imagine trying to explain its benefits to an alien who is ignorant of Earth life. How could their questions and reactions show up the absurdity of the subject?

SUMMING UP
- Sketches contain the fundamentals of most kinds of comedy.
- The two main types are the idea sketch and the character sketch.
- You can create premises for idea sketches by juxtaposing different elements of reality.

2
WRITING SKETCHES: BUILDING YOUR IDEAS

You have a brilliant idea for a sketch. But what happens when you need to write a second? You can't just go back to where you got it and pick another one. Even the most successful comedy writers don't go through their day in a blaze of inspiration with brilliant ideas exploding in their mind. Most of the time, inspiration comes from work. There are techniques you can use to get your brain into gear and get those ideas popping, even when you're feeling flat and uncreative.

OPENING UP A FLOW OF IDEAS

If you wanted to buy shoes, you wouldn't go into a shop that sold just the one pair: you'd find somewhere with a range of designs and then make your mind up. It's the same when you're looking for comedy concepts. You need to find a broad base of potential material from which your ideas can spring. Once you've done that groundwork you can look at the possibilities and pick the most promising. That way, you'll have several embryonic ideas to choose from: if you discard one, you can look at another. Just like buying shoes.

At the same time, our brains seem to work better when we limit our focus. When scouring the universe, our minds can become confused and overloaded. We work more productively when we concentrate on something concrete. We need to find a finite and specific theme, and then open it up to discover its widest possibilities.

You can't wait for inspiration. You have to go after it with a club.

Jack London

USING IDEAGRAMS

These are a great way for comedy writers to get ideas. There's nothing simpler. First pick a theme and then break it down into topics, which you spread out over a page or on your screen. You can now cast your eyes up and down the sheet or screen to find possibilities.

The value of ideagrams is that they're visual. This stimulates your brain more effectively than thinking up ideas cerebrally. Ideagrams work laterally, freeing the mind more than linear lists. The spread-out design enables you to join up things that aren't normally connected, so you can work more creatively. Here's how you do it.

FIRST PICK A THEME

Think of something you want to write about. For the sake of this exercise let's choose that great sketch subject, 'Eating Out'. See Figure 1.

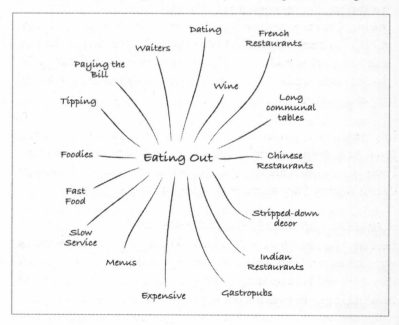

Figure 1

BREAK THE THEME DOWN INTO TOPICS

- *Spread the topics outwards from the main theme*: write the theme in the centre of the page. Now surround it with as many aspects of it as you can think of. Cover the page with them. You'll come out with something similar to Figure 1.
- *Don't judge your efforts*: don't try too hard to be funny. You're not writing comedy just yet – you're just building the foundations. Think up as many topics of the theme as you can; you're jotting down facts rather than trying to create hilarity.
- *Choose an everyday subject*: choose something mundane to which people can relate. You may have an impressive knowledge of quantum physics, but the audience won't get the jokes. Also, avoid something abstract like 'Greed': it's a major part of human nature but it's very conceptual. We're looking for a more physical theme. On the other hand, avoid something too specific. 'Clock Golf', I'm sure, contains comedy possibilities but they're likely to run out quite quickly. 'Sport', less funny in itself, will offer a far wider range while still being concrete and quotidian. Like, of course, 'Eating Out'.

In Figure 1 we have sixteen topics derived from 'Eating Out'. I could have written more but this is enough with which to start. Some of the topics are very general, others are matters of detail. It doesn't matter. They all relate in some way to the theme.

NOW BREAK YOUR TOPICS DOWN INTO SUBTOPICS

Let's try 'Waiters'. It's a rich subject. Think of the many different types of waiter, both male and female, the diverse ways in which they dress and behave, and anything relevant to their world. Spread these subtopics outwards from the topic as I've done in Figure 2.

You see how we're going into more detail. This is a high-calibre comedy weapon. The more minute the focus of your sketch, the more effective it can be. Detail feeds both originality and realism. Generality is the enemy of comedy. Now's the time to see if we can glean any ideas from all this groundwork.

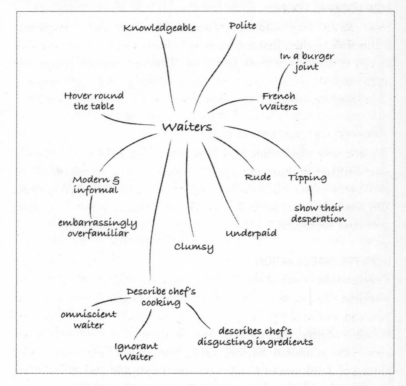

Figure 2

TURNING A TOPIC INTO A COMEDY IDEA

PICK A SUBTOPIC AND TRY TO JUXTAPOSE IT

Let's look at 'French waiters'. They create an instant image. What happens if we place an elegant French waiter in a burger joint? Can we visualize any possibilities? Imagine the waiter trying to explain to a customer how the burger is flipped as if they were in a gourmet restaurant. Either jot it down by the subtopic or on a separate sheet, as you see in Figure 2.

KEEP LOOKING ROUND

How about very informal waiters? The types who introduce themselves by their first name, dress in jeans and a T-shirt, and talk to you as if you were their best mate. They're a very contemporary phenomenon, which adds to their comedy value. It seems a promising area. Let's jot that down as well.

IF AT FIRST YOU DON'T SUCCEED . . .

You probably won't come up with any sure-fire, gold-plated ideas in your first few minutes of work. At this stage, you're more likely to have two or three half-formed concepts that may or may not work. You won't know that until later. Be patient and keep on looking over your subtopics.

NOW TRY EXAGGERATION

Exaggeration is one of the simplest and most effective tools in your workbox. First find a promising subtopic. Is there anything in it you can profitably puff up? A great example of an exaggeration sketch is Monty Python's 'Four Yorkshiremen'. Four old men bicker about the supposed hardships of their youth. They start with having to drink out of a rolled-up newspaper and end with licking the road clean before being stabbed to death by their dad.

The overfamiliar waiter seems to be ripe for this. He could begin with the usual, 'Hi, my name's Martin, how's your day been?' and go on to pull up a chair and insist that the diners exchange embarrassing personal confidences with him. The tension could build as he tries to make them come up with increasingly excruciating confessions.

If something occurs to you, jot it down or mark it with a highlighter pen – or do both. I'll put down 'embarrassingly overfamiliar'. It's something to return to later.

TRY PARODY

Can you express a topic in the form of a movie, a novel or some other art form? Right away, I can think of a couple of famous movie restaurant scenes: the fake orgasm in *When Harry Met Sally*, and Joe Pesci's threatening 'Funny how? I mean, funny like I'm a clown?' speech in *Goodfellas*. How could we play with these? If they took place in a different kind of restaurant, how would the waiter behave?

TRY REVERSAL

This is another time-honoured trick. Is there any way by which the situation can be overturned, turned inside-out or reversed?

A famous example of this is the *Goodness Gracious Me* team's 'Going for an English' sketch, which I mentioned in the previous chapter. A group of people in Bombay (as it was then called) go out for a meal in an English restaurant. They're drunk, they abuse and patronize the waiter, and generally behave obnoxiously. They boast about ordering the blandest thing on the menu. Everything that happens in the sketch is a straightforward reversal of Brits going out for an Indian meal.

Look around your subtopics. What can be reversed? One of my students, using the 'Dating' topic, wrote a sketch about a restaurant which, instead of laying on a special romantic table for Valentine's Day, had an argument table for divorcing couples. Naturally, the wine was sour, the waiter and waitress encouraged flirtation, and when the bill came the woman's items were four times more expensive than the man's.

LOOK AT THE BEHAVIOUR

For every human activity, there's a socially accepted way of going about things. It's called manners. We make social transactions much easier by following agreed patterns of conduct. These codes are a heaven-sent opportunity for comedy writers to subvert.

Everything on the ideagram involves typical behaviour. For example, waiters in high-class restaurants can be keen to tell diners about the marvellous skills of the chef. How can we twist this? We could try a reversal: maybe they don't describe the delicious ingredients but the chef's disgusting habits.

Or we could exaggerate the waiter's omniscience as he progresses from the ingredients to the molecular secrets of the universe. Or, in a reversal, he could be so ignorant he has to ask the diner what's on the plate. These are just possibilities but it's worth jotting them down and highlighting them.

Another subtopic is 'Tipping'. It's a touchy issue. Waiters are normally self-effacing about it, as if it didn't really matter to them. What if one let the mask slip and showed how desperate they were for a few extra quid? For every situation, think of the social rules involved and see how you can break them.

FOLLOW YOUR INSTINCTS

If a voice in your head tells you strongly that something is funny or potentially funny, listen to it. Comedy's personal. Your own experience and psychological makeup should have a powerful bearing on the topics you write about, and how you write about them.

Exercise

Make an ideagram based on a theme of your choice. Fill a page with it. Break down at least three of the topics into subtopics.

→ **NOW TRY THIS**

Keep all your ideagrams in your computer or a ring file, labelled according to theme. Refer to them again whenever you want ideas.

OTHER WAYS OF GETTING IDEAS

DON'T TREAT THESE TIPS AS RULES

All the techniques we've been looking at are just that – techniques. Their sole purpose is to turn on those light bulbs in your brain. Many writers find them helpful. However, if you're still struggling with them after several tries, don't sweat. There are plenty of ways to tickle your mind and get into that elusive comedy mindset. The only rule when looking for comedy ideas is to do what works best for you.

A combination of methods often does the trick. Give yourself a variety of tools in your box that feel comfortable to use. When your mind feels stale after working with one of them, pick up another. Some days you may find ideagrams really helpful, on others another method works better. The human mind is highly complex and we're all different. Through trial and error find your favourite idea-finding methods and learn how to mix and match them.

Here are some other ways of kick-starting your brain.

LOOK IN MAGAZINES AND NEWSPAPERS

- *Treat press articles as you would an ideagram*: there's always a wealth of material in newspapers and magazines. If your budget is an issue the good news is that, often, the cheaper the publication, the more fruitful the possibilities.

- *Try reversing the topic of an article*: right now I'm flicking through an inexpensive weekly colour gossip magazine. There's a lot of comedy potential here. There are two articles about women triumphing over dangerous diseases and accidents. They're written to inspire the readers and I'm not laughing at that. But what if I had a man triumphing over man flu? There are also some recipes for healthy lunchtime snacks for your kids. I could try a reversal with recipes for the kind of health-destroying goo that kids really like.

- *Try juxtaposition and exaggeration*: bring to bear all the techniques you picked up earlier in the chapter to draw comedy ideas out of the articles.
- *Use visuals*: photos and drawings are as valuable a source as written articles.
- *Don't expect everything to work*: my magazine also has a photo of a rabbit that has won a 'Cute Bunny' contest and there's a column by someone who analyses readers' dreams. Nothing springs to mind at the moment (which is not to say it won't tomorrow).

LOOK AT TV

Television shouts at us what's in the air and is always a topic of conversation. Keep a jotting pad with you as you watch. It could be the news, a game show, a drama, a soap. Can you spot anything you can exaggerate, juxtapose or reverse?

LOOK AT ADVERTS

The same goes for print ads and TV and radio commercials. Being visual, they can spark ideas off wonderfully. They communicate directly and are full of attitudes to life.

USE A NOTEBOOK

If you don't already have a small pad nestling in your bag or breast pocket, get one. Make it a small one that you can whip out quickly when inspiration strikes, which often happens when we're thinking of something completely different. You need to be ready. An idea can come at an awkward moment and vanish as quickly as it came. Don't bank on remembering it until you get home: write it down immediately or at the first chance.

IT TAKES PRACTICE

There isn't a single aspect of writing that comes easily at first, except maybe turning on your computer. Making ideagrams, finding ideas and writing dialogue and jokes are all complicated cerebral activities involving countless brain cells whirring at astronomical speeds. It's not surprising that your first few shots at them may be tricky. Don't beat yourself up if you can't come up with ideas of genius right from the start.

Create an ideagram or two, make notes from magazines and find your own ways of stimulating your brain for comedy. Persist. Sooner or later the ideas will flow.

> **→ NOW TRY THIS**
>
> When you're in a public place watch how people behave. What facets of their behaviour strike you as interesting or funny? How can these be exaggerated? How can they be juxtaposed with a different situation or with a different person? Use your notebook.

THE SQUARE PEG

You can create comedy by simply placing somebody in a situation for which they're totally unsuited or untrained and envisaging the chaos that ensues. Use the upturned situation to bring out the worst characteristics in your misplaced person or the unfortunate people they encounter.

You can create square-peg situations by making a list of jobs and professions, and then another of personal qualities. Don't strain, just jot them down as they occur to you. Look at Figure 3. Both these lists were written quickly and automatically.

• *Mix and mismatch*: simply join random words from the Jobs and Adjectives lists until you find a pairing that has comic possibilities. Add to the lists or make your own. The point is to put someone in a position in which they're a fish out of water and see what mayhem ensues. Have fun by breaking the rules of

JOBS		ADJECTIVES	
Bishop	Opera Singer	Happy	Disapproving
Portrait Photographer	Pig Farmer	Stupid	Repetitive
Submarine Captain	Obituary Writer	Jealous	Hard-working
Hairdresser	Porn Star	Lecherous	French
Call Centre Worker	All-In Wrestler	Hypochondriac	Tired
Secret Agent	Masseuse	Genius	Talks in questions
Terrorist	Chef	Jocular	Rural
Shop Assistant	Gravedigger	Furious	Childish
Art Gallery Attendant	Poet	Slow	Contradictory
Waiter	Professor	Think they're funny	Negative
Abattoir Worker	Surgeon	Boring	Energetic
Dentist	Football Commentator	Depressed	Monosyllabic
Train Driver	War Reporter	Pedantic	Nervous
Doctor's Receptionist	Zoo Keeper	Distracted	Intellectual
Decorator	Postman	Pompous	Violent
Window Cleaner	Fighter Pilot	Overfamiliar	Paranoid
Lollipop Lady	Dustman	In pain	Snobbish
Pickpocket	Hypnotherapist	Philosophical	Eager to please
Traffic Warden	Merchant Banker	Courteous	Touchy-feely
Chat Show Host	Tour Guide	Over-technical	Homesick

Figure 3

conventional behaviour. Remember that a lot of the humour will spring from the reactions of the other characters.

- *Discover the comedy in the situation*: say you've chosen a depressed dentist. Doctors and dentists have great comedy potential: a lot could be at stake for the patient and there's the enticing prospect of pain. So what's funny here? Depressed people can be bound up with their difficult thought processes. He or she could be very unalert. They could terrify the patient as they hold the drill near their mouth. Other aspects of the operation could be fun: injections, applying the amalgam, taking X-rays.
- *Develop the idea into a story*: maybe we now have an embryonic sketch premise. Now's the time to see whether it will hold up. Remember that a sketch tells a story. What's the action of the sketch?

Let's try a subtly different scenario. Maybe the dentist is an existentially despairing Hamlet philosopher-type and the patient has a raging toothache. The more the patient complains, the more the dentist tells them that pain is the essence of human existence and must be borne. As he witters on he becomes less able to wield the drill, convincing him/herself that all action is hopeless faced with an indifferent universe . . .

You get the picture. We've made a few decisions: the reason for the depression (philosophy) and the urgency of the patient's problem. There's a situation which will build to a head – a story in the making. There are other possible reasons for the depression (the dentist is losing their job, their partner has left, etc.) but this idea seems promising.

Of course, we're trying to milk laughs from a condition that is far from funny for those suffering it. Comedy is often based on someone's pain. We'll look at this issue a little later.

→ **NOW TRY THIS**

Once a week flick through your notebook to see what you've recorded. Open a file of idea possibilities and transfer any that look promising. Refer to this file regularly and ask which of the ideas could be developed. Sometimes things you passed over today look good a month later.

The premise is the idea that drives the sketch. It is usual to get this across early. It can be absurd but sometimes the premise quite ordinary. E.g. 'Some people are always finishing off the sentences of others' is a perfectly adequate premise. There's nothing exotic about this idea, it's observation of human behaviour by someone with a notebook.

Peter Vincent, writer on *The Two Ronnies*
and BBC sitcoms including *Sorry!*

THE IMPORTANCE OF GETTING A RANGE OF IDEAS

By now you may be itching to get to work on your sketch. You're maybe wondering why we're holding back from the 'real' part of the process – the writing. But it's vital that you learn early how to produce a quantity of ideas. All this is as much 'real writing' as setting down the dialogue.

SUBMITTING IN BULK

Writing just one or two sketches won't cut it. This may seem harsh, until you talk to a comedy producer. They'll tell you stories about wannabe writers who submit the same sketch over and over again in the hope that someone, someday, will recognize their genius. It doesn't work like that.

Your value as a comedy writer will depend on your ability to keep on coming up with ideas of a consistent standard. It takes more than talent to maintain this work rate and consistency. Techniques such as the ones you've been learning will help your brain work regularly (as well as creatively) in this way.

NOT ALL IDEAS WORK

To be blunt, don't always trust your self-assessment of your creations. You may sweat for hours over what you know to be a work of comedy genius to find it looks very weak the next day. The piece you eventually sell may well be that third-rate idea you were about to throw in the bin.

PRACTISE GETTING IDEAS

It's worth taking time to flex your creative muscles and build numerous comedy worlds. Over time you'll be able to write sketch after sketch of a decent standard on a variety of topics and in different styles. That's when you'll find yourself in demand. So hang on in there, try your hand at all the methods I've described and even come up with some of your own.

GIVING OFFENCE

One of the most common anxieties of new comedy writers is the extent to which you can be cruel, use swear words or laugh at people's religion, beliefs, gender and sexuality. What are the rights and wrongs?

BE AWARE OF YOUR AUDIENCE

Let's look at it in a different light. Most of the time you'll be aiming your work at a specific outlet: radio, TV, or maybe a local comedy club. Does your target show regularly feature four-letter words and jokes about bodily functions? If it's the BBC, it almost certainly doesn't. Radio has hundreds of thousands of listeners and TV millions of viewers who include families and people far more conservative views than the producers and writers. An audience of half-drunk punters in a comedy club at 10.30 p.m. will be much more relaxed about language and content.

BE AWARE OF CHANGING ATTITUDES

These days you do hear 'fuck' on post-watershed shows. Some programmes use scatological material unthinkable twenty years ago. In other areas, attitudes have become much more censorious. Forty years ago in old-fashioned working men's clubs it would have been acceptable to call people 'poofs' or 'Pakis'. It isn't any more. However, these days gay people often refer to themselves as 'queers' and straight people use 'gay' as a mildly and jokily pejorative word. It's all become a bit of a minefield.

BE AWARE OF YOUR INTENT

Few people will be upset if you create a comic jihadist. But if you seem to imply that all Muslims are bombers then you could be in trouble. The line between humorous comment and prejudicial rant can be hard to see at times, but as comedy writers we need to know in our own minds where it lies.

However, cruelty and rudeness are an essential part of comedy. Most jokes involve a victim of some kind. Giving offence is part of the give and take of an open society, and comedy plays a crucial role in this. Be as offensive or as rude as you need to be, no more and no less, while being fully aware of the constraints on the producers. Laugh at people's religion or background, by all means, but make it truthful and realize that they may be upset. The worst pitfall is being misunderstood. Jimmy Carr, no stranger to giving perceived offence, sets out a good rule: if you have to look over your shoulder, don't tell the joke.

AVOID CRUDITY FOR ITS OWN SAKE

Being crude is not the same as being funny. When I've staged sketch shows I'm often mildly depressed by the proportion of writers who think that the merest mention of penises and farts is hilarious. It's not. As a rule, if you're writing for a mainstream broadcaster, avoid crude humour unless you can be really original and fresh. There's a wealth of all kinds of material in the real world out there, as I hope we're beginning to find out.

Exercise

Come up with three sketch ideas, one from your ideagram topics, another from the square-peg list and another inspired by something in the press. Think the ideas through and, in three or four sentences, describe each premise and how you see it unfolding. Don't write the full sketches just yet. Which idea seems most promising?

TROUBLESHOOTING

'I've gone over the ideagram and tried all the techniques but still can't come up with any funny ideas.'

Take a break: maybe you're suffering from the writer's number one enemy – the inner voice that snaps 'That's not funny!' at you. It shouts loudest when you're tired or stressed. Give your brain a rest, overnight if need be, and then come back.

Have you broken your ideagram down into enough subtopics? The more detail you create, the more chances you give yourself.

Ask more questions. Think of this poem by Kipling:

I keep six honest serving-men,
(They taught me all I knew);
Their names are What and Why and When
And How and Where and Who.

Kipling knew a thing or two about writing. Let's try his advice. Imagine your topic is 'offices'. As a subtopic, maybe you've jotted down those cuddly felt mascots people place on their desk. Try a reversal: imagine a woman at work who, instead of a cute fluffy animal, displays an ugly baboon-type ape.

Ask 'Why?' Maybe the ugly animal represents her ex-boyfriend. Maybe she's stuck pins into it and pasted a photo of the man's face on to the ape's head. Ask 'Where?' She's clearly in the office, at work. If it's open plan, we can see the people near her. Ask 'Who are they?' Maybe the woman at the next desk has a similar ugly mascot. Maybe it has the same face glued to it. Maybe both of the mascots have a note attached saying 'James – lousy cheat'. We can guess what's been going on.

Keep on asking these questions. They may well spark off ideas which lead to a sketch.

'I don't want to bother with ideagrams and all this juxtaposing and reversing stuff. I just want to write a sketch about this crazy character I know.'

If you want to use something or someone from your everyday life, that's great. But you still need to twist round or reframe the person to create comedy. If you try to write directly from your own experience, that which seems hilarious to you could leave the audience cold.

Find a way of abstracting your subject matter from your own life so people can relate to it. So turn 'Fran, my unbearably rude colleague' into a topic: 'Rude people at work'. Then try exaggerating it, juxtaposing it, reversing it or looking at it through whatever lens seems to work. The result may stray quite a bit from Fran but it's much more likely to make people laugh.

SUMMING UP
- You can create a base of material for sketch ideas by making an ideagram on a topic.
- You can turn the material into comedy ideas by using juxtaposition, exaggeration or reversal.
- You can also get ideas by putting people into inappropriate situations.

- To submit sketches, you need to be able to come up with a flow of ideas.
- To avoid worry about giving offence, think about who will be watching your comedy and be clear about your intentions.

3
WRITING SKETCHES: BUILDING THE STRUCTURE

Planning doesn't mean cutting out spontaneity. On the contrary, it's when you are confident about your direction that your mind can really take flight. Uncertainty chokes inspiration.

FIRMING UP YOUR PREMISE

- What is the premise of the sketch?
- Can you describe the premise in a sentence?
- Does it hold possibilities?
- Can you visualize the story developing over a couple of minutes?

Keep the answers to these questions firmly in your vision as you continue to build the sketch. If you're struggling to find them, go over your concept again and see if you can make it work.

ESTABLISHING THE LOCATION AND STORY

WHERE ARE WE?
Often, the sketch idea itself makes the choice. Choose the location that best brings out the conflict. The 'Disgusting Chef' idea from the last chapter obviously takes place in a restaurant. If we make it a very high-class joint, the expectations of the diners will be higher and their reactions will be stronger.

WHAT HAPPENS?

- *Establish what is going on at the beginning*: a sketch, above all, tells a story. What's going on? In the 'Disgusting Chef' idea from the previous chapter the action is clear: the waiter's in the early stages of taking the order.

- *How is the situation exacerbated?* Your sketch will exaggerate or overturn reality in some way. In 'Disgusting Chef' the waiter can describe the chef's cooking methods and the diners will be shocked. This could build through the starter and into the main, as his descriptions become increasingly gruesome. I envisage the chef coming out into the restaurant to up the ante – anything to add action and conflict.

ESTABLISHING THE CHARACTERS

WHO'S IN IT?

Establish who's there. Keep numbers down but use enough people to build the momentum. In 'Disgusting Chef' I'll make the diners a dating couple. The man's trying to impress the woman with his knowledge of food. This should lead to some enjoyable tension. I'll add the waiter and the chef to make four characters.

You should still be ready to change the concept, location and characters of your sketch. Things are not yet set in stone. If you've a gut feeling something isn't completely right with your premise, go back and rework it.

WHAT ARE THEY LIKE?

- *Avoid ciphers*: give each character a personality, albeit a simple, cartoony one. In 'Disgusting Chef' I see the waiter as pretentiously French. The male diner is keen to impress the woman. She's sceptical and less tolerant of what goes on; the chef is belligerent and scary. As we continue writing, all this could be tweaked. However, once you've established their characteristic, stick to it like glue. If they're conniving and slippery, for example, that's what they are throughout.
- *Give them names*: this will help fix them in your imagination and will get the reader into the situation quicker. 'Mrs Brown' and 'Julie' looks much better than 'Woman 1' and 'Woman 2', even

if the audience never finds out their names. I'll call my male diner Piers and his wife Amanda. The waiter remains just Waiter.

- *Use types*: whether we like it or not, most of us belong to an overall type. Opinionated taxi drivers, patronizing know-it-alls, screaming party girls – they all exist and they're us. It may not be fair, but stereotyping is meat and drink to comedy, as long as it reflects reality. It creates an invaluable shorthand that the audience can read immediately. Every profession has its own types: jargon-spouting IT workers, wolf-whistling builders, inarticulate models. Use these with glee and exaggerate them shamelessly. But beware – they can date quickly.

- *Use uniforms*: you have no time to explain your characters. An official uniform, such as a policeman's or nurse's, or an unofficial one, like the baseball cap and trainers of a street kid, gives the audience an immediate clue about the character and what they're up to.

> **→ NOW TRY THIS**
> When dreaming up your characters, try describing them to yourself with an adjective such as 'Mrs Frustrated', 'Mr Stuffy', etc. It'll help you characterize them to yourself. Keep it simple and one-dimensional: there's no time for layering and development.

The development explores the premise further. If the premise does not respond to development, abandon the idea. Think of a better premise. The law of diminishing returns is waiting to gobble up the unwary humorist. This law rears its ugly head when the writer forgets to write 'story' into his work.

Peter Vincent

BUILDING THE STRUCTURE

Sketches have three parts:

- The setup;
- The build;
- The ending.

WRITING THE SETUP

If the audience don't get your premise within the first few seconds, the sketch is in danger of floundering. Establish the concept, situation and characters within the first three or four speeches or actions, as well as any comic tropes that will give the piece flavour.

WRITING THE BUILD

This is the heart of the sketch, in which you bring the premise to fruition. You have a couple of minutes to build the idea and incorporate as many laughs as possible. It's a good idea (again) to go back to your original concept and make sure it's simple, funny and has 'sketch legs'.

- *Build the conflict*: you're telling a story, and story reveals conflict. Is there something going on that raises the stakes for your characters? What is the issue that sets them against each other? They don't need to pull knives on each other. But they do need to gnaw with increasing fervour at the bone of contention between them. So, is there a little bit of extra jeopardy you can add to the mix? Stay within the logic of the piece. And don't take it too far: if every sketch involved a fight we'd soon feel as battered as the characters. In 'Disgusting Chef', friction could develop between the diners as the waiter reveals the horrible content of the meal: she's appalled while he's rather impressed. When she gets stroppy the chef can come out holding a cleaver. There's an element of threat now.

- *Avoid 'Talking Heads'*: a common reason why a sketch fails is because nothing happens in it. Typically, there are two blokes in a pub (it's usually blokes) talking about something that happened yesterday or about a third bloke. The banter may be amusing but after about half a minute it becomes really dull. The topic is offstage or in the past. Nothing's at stake. Peter Cook and Dudley Moore made this kind of piece their signature, but their chemistry was extraordinary. You should ensure that something is going on and there's conflict.

BUILDING IN THE LAUGHS

- *Get the laughs*: conflict isn't funny in itself. A man returns a dead pet to the pet shop and is told by the assistant that it isn't really dead. It sounds sad, even tragic. What made the parrot sketch funny was the extraordinary performance of John Cleese. And while your premise may be amusing, you will probably need to do some extra work to get consistent laughs. A two-minute sketch needs at least six good laughs. You need to maintain and build comic momentum at every line. To do that, you need jokes. By these, I simply mean moments when the audience laughs. These could be funny things your characters say or visual gags. Quite a few of them may have come into your head when you dreamt up the premise. They should all spring directly from the situation and the characters and not feel as if you've shoehorned them in. But they must come frequently and regularly. As with most things in comedy writing, a few techniques will make the job much easier.
- *Make a list*: build a list of moments or lines when you expect to get a laugh. A lot of the humour in 'Disgusting Chef' will come from replacing the finely prepared elements of haute cuisine with things found in a health-hazard kitchen. Researching for ideas, I looked at the menus of Michelin-starred restaurants on the internet and made a short list:

- Confit de Canard
- Salad
- Fennel
- Light Broth
- Croutons
- Bouillabaisse
- Ragout
- Smoked

Once I'd done that, I made another list. This one was of nasty things that could be found in unclean kitchens:

- Dust
- Burnt oven scrapings
- Cockroaches
- Packets of out-of-date food
- Grease
- Mould
- Flaking plaster/paint

I could make both lists quite a bit longer but they're enough to be getting on with. What happens if we mismatch elements from each one? Oven scrapings could be dished up like croutons. Mould could be part of a green salad. I think the cockroaches could go in anywhere. Smoked items on the menu could become the ash from a chef's cigarette. Dust could be sprinkled over, literally as a 'dusting'. So, I have five potential laughs already. If I lengthened the lists and made more juxtapositions I could add more.

- *Reincorporate.* Try bringing back something that was said or done earlier on in the sketch. You can deliberately plant something early on so you can refer to it or repeat it later. Don't overdo this, though. Unless you're writing a sketch based on . . .
- *Repetition.* This is a wonderful comic standby. It breaks a fundamental rule of comedy – that it should be constantly surprising (which goes to show, of course, that there are no rules).

Simply repeat a phrase or an action over and over and you can create delicious expectations. You need to find the right phrase and not overdo it.

- *Avoid writing to your own formula.* Nothing falls flatter than a sketch that is written as if by numbers. Making lists is a great help when you're building up the laughs, but make sure your sketch tells a story and is more than just a shopping list of jokes. One of my students wrote a sketch about a boss explaining the office rules to a new employee. These were weird: staff were expected to throw orange peel at each other at every opportunity, from brainstorming sessions and coffee breaks to meetings. It's an enjoyable idea, but after half a page of jokes about peel and pips it became very flat. After a rewrite, the new employee became the cleaner who was expected to clear all the mess up. Tension was introduced, there was more drama and the sketch became alive.

- *Use the rule of three.* This is a long-standing comedy axiom that persists because it's true. There's something about a rhythm of three which is at the heart of comedy. The first phrase, word or action introduces the idea; the second sets the rhythm; by the time we reach the third, the audience have got the idea and they laugh. The third repetition, however, can also undermine the pattern rather than simply confirm it, which is another very good way of getting laughs.

- *Think visually.* A visual gag can be as funny as a verbal one and can be established instantly. All through the sketch, try to give your characters funny things to do as well as say. Think how you can use:
  - *Actions*: are there any funny physical reactions you can give your characters? Can you replace a line or two with a movement or a gesture?
  - *Props*: is there anything in the location that can be picked up, used or just bumped into? Restaurants are full of these, not least the food. In a doctor's surgery, for example, there are stethoscopes, rubber gloves, syringes . . .

○ *Clothes*: do your characters wear anything which can be incorporated?

Sketches are often set up visually. At the beginning ask, 'What can the audience see?' You may be able to establish everything you need at the bat of an eyelid without any dialogue. The use of uniforms and instantly recognizable locations will help you here. There are many settings, such as doctor's surgeries, restaurants and ticket offices, that give the audience vital clues to what's going on.

Always bear in mind, though, that you must keep everything within the logic and the action of the sketch. Adding extraneous jokes, visual or verbal, that don't belong weakens your premise and is a turn-off.

→ NOW TRY THIS

Pick up a nearby object. Look at it and touch it. Think of a purpose for it which is not its designed use. Can you create comedy from this? Think of anything that might be lying around in your sketch set. What 'new' purposes could it be put to?

Exercise

Look at a couple of sketches on TV, the radio or the internet. Ask yourself whether the tension mounts as the sketch develops, and how the writer has done this.

WRITING THE ENDING

You've packed in six good laughs or, with a bit of luck, ten. You've built up the tension nicely, and above all you've got a great premise to which you've stuck closely. The sketch is looking good. But how do you finish it? You don't want to jeopardize all your good work with a weak finish.

- *Endings are the continuity*: if an ending's weak, there'll be a sag in energy, which will carry over into the next sketch. Often, the type of endings used colours the style of a sketch show.
- *Construct your endings deliberately*: sometimes the ending will flow naturally from within the sketch itself, in which case you're lucky. It's more common to write a sketch with a nagging feeling you don't know how it will finish. You need to take some time to find one that works.
- *Types of ending*: this list is far from comprehensive. You can do your own research and add some of your own.
    - The Rollover: The Groundhog Day scenario, when we know the situation is going to be repeated over and over. In the impressions show *Dead Ringers*, two TV historians analysed a battle re-enactment – fought between their own camera crews. As the losing side scattered, we saw Tony Robinson's *Time Team* crew looming threateningly on the ridge. This kind of ending only works with certain sketches, but if you can pull it off, it's a winner.
    - Reincorporation: Simply bring back into the sketch something that was said or done earlier on.
    - The Reveal: A little old-fashioned these days, but worth a look. We find we've been misled as to what's been going on – and discover the truth. Reveals are usually done visually, e.g. 'THE CAMERA PULLS BACK TO REVEAL THAT THE MAN IN THE PORTER'S UNIFORM IS ACTUALLY PLAYING WITH HIS TOY TRAIN IN HIS BEDROOM.'
    - The Big Laugh: If you simply end up on a really good laugh the sketch will at least have gone out with a bang. If they laugh loud enough the audience won't worry that there hasn't been a 'proper' ending.
    - The Natural End: The events have a natural culmination. For example, if someone in a bus queue is trapped in conversation with a weird stranger you can simply end it when the bus

comes. But do find something funny, visually or verbally, for the final grace note.

o The Mad Road Sign: Events go off in a different and unexpected direction. It's related to the Rollover, except it's less logical.

o The Fizzle Away: Things just splutter to a halt and fade away. It has a cinematic feel and is more like real life.

Every show has its own style of ending the sketches. Crazy links wouldn't have worked in *Smack the Pony*. Non-endings wouldn't fit in broad shows like *The Armstrong & Miller Show*. However, when you start submitting your sketches, try to vary the kind of finish you use. Show your versatility.

No beginner should write without an outline. Most writing problems – psychological barriers, setbacks, disappointments – come from the absence of a proper outline.

Ayn Rand, writer

Exercise

Look at the list of three sketch ideas that you made at the end of the last chapter. Using the skills you have learnt above, envisage a story and characters for each of them. If it doesn't seem to work, put the idea aside and move to the next one. Highlight the idea that you feel has the most promise.

TROUBLESHOOTING

'I don't see how I can build the conflict. My sketch is about two women chatting under the hairdryers. It's dialogue-based and not much happens.'

There will be conflict at some level. It needn't be melodramatic or overt. Maybe the two characters have a subtly different philosophy. If they do talk as one, they'll be set against the rest of the world in some way. Conversation can express conflict as much as direct action can. Say they are discussing a magazine article they are both reading. Their opinions on it may be vastly polarized or only a hair's breadth apart. The audience will be interested in that hair's breadth, so develop and intensify it, even if only by a shade. If the subject of the conversation is in the past or offstage, make sure we see the impact on the two characters in the here and now. We need to see something actually happening before our eyes or the sketch is dramatically dead.

SUMMING UP

- To structure your sketch, you need to establish the location, the characters and the story.
- The setup must be established quickly and clearly.
- The sketch needs to build with some kind of escalating drama.
- There are many ways to end a sketch. It's good to practise a variety.
- Think visually and be unpredictable.

4
WRITING SKETCHES: DIALOGUE AND REWRITING

Your preparation will make you progress much faster and with more confidence as you settle down to write your sketch. For the time being, use a standard stage layout with the characters' names on the left and the dialogue tabbed a few spaces to the right. Place any actions separately between the speeches.

It's important that you tell yourself that this is just the first draft. You can't expect to create beautifully honed lines, hilarious jokes and perfect comedy rhythm at the first shot. Everything you see and hear on TV and radio will have been pored over, gone through, rubbed out and reworked many times. First drafts are always imperfect, even clumsy. Everything can be put right when you come back later and thoroughly rework it.

If there's one comment I've never heard, especially if people have found the sketch funny, it's this one: 'That was too short.'

Jon Wolanske, member of San Francisco
sketch group Killing My Lobster

WRITING DIALOGUE

- *Use everyday speech*: however surreal your comedy world, the people who inhabit it will overwhelmingly be everyday twenty-first-century folk. Your characters can be as inarticulate as you like as long as the audience understands them. If you're writing a sketch set in the past, use a neutral but everyday language – unless you're doing, say, a Charlotte Brontë spoof, in which case exaggerate the speech unashamedly, having, of course, studied the dialogue in one of her novels.

- *Be brief*: less is always more. Long speeches are anathema to modern comedy. Write the dialogue quite quickly and go back over it again and again, cutting out the dead wood. You'll be amazed at how much you can tighten it after a couple of drafts. Watch out for:
  - Unnecessary words: 'Didn't we all have a brilliant time together during last Tuesday night?' could immediately be cut to 'We all had a great time last Tuesday night!' It's still a bit clunky. You could compress it to 'Tuesday night – great, eh?'
  - Repetitions: in the line quoted above, for example, 'all' and 'together' give us the same information. Get rid of the longer word. Watch out, too, for repeated information. This really annoys the audience, who are better at picking things up than you think.
  - Length of the speech: if it's more than four lines, it's probably too long.
- *Be emotional*: if all your characters do is pass information on to each other, the dialogue will be bone dry. Every human communication contains emotion. Understand what your characters are feeling and show this through the words they speak.
- *Incorporate reactions*: when writing dialogue, imagine the reactions of the characters who aren't talking. This can add hugely to the comedy. You can build in more laughs without adding any more words.
- *Be in character*: characterization should shine through your dialogue. Has *everyone* in your cast got a distinct manner of speaking? There are plenty of ways to reveal a character through their speech. For example:
  - Pedantic/pompous. Use an extended grammatical structure with subordinate clauses (and even parenthetical interpolations);
  - Brusque/blunt. Simple sentences and short words. Active verbs;

- Angry. Emphatic language, exclamation marks. Even CAPITAL LETTERS;
- Diffident. Sentences hang in a sort of, well . . . um. End sentences with question marks?
- Professional jargon. Think of the vocabulary and the style of speech of different professions.

> **→ NOW TRY THIS**
> Place the part of the line that gets the laugh at the end of the speech. That way the audience's laughter won't cover information they may need.

TRUST YOUR LUCK

Don't plan everything to the nth degree. Give rein to your instincts and feel as relaxed and loose as you can. If something unexpected happens, or a random speech pops into your head, try it out. It may well work: some of your funniest writing will come when you least expect it.

Exercise

Now look at your most promising idea from the exercise in the last chapter. Write it out as a complete sketch, as fast as you can. Revise it several times.

REWRITING THE SKETCH

Whether it took you minutes or hours to complete the sketch, you will certainly need to go over it again. Each draft will be better than the last. Do at least three of them.

READ THE SKETCH OUT ALOUD

What may look great on the page can sound clumsy and stilted when spoken. Read your words out aloud at performance pace, even if you don't think of yourself as an actor.

CHECKLIST

- The original idea: have you followed it closely without going off on a tangent?
- The beginning: is your premise set up in no more than four speeches or actions?
- The length: if you've covered over three pages of A4, it's probably too long.
- The number of characters: if you've more than four, try to cut some of them or amalgamate two into one.
- The location: does everything happen in just one place?
- The dialogue: cut it back. Then go back again and cut it further. There's no such thing as a sketch that can't be trimmed further, even after twenty rewrites.
- The laughs: a two-minute sketch should have a minimum of six proper laughs (as opposed to chuckles). Use the red/green highlighter method below to check.
- The ending: is it satisfying and funny?

> **→ NOW TRY THIS**
> Go back over your dialogue and highlight in red lines that are designed to get a laugh. Highlight in green the lines that are a direct build-up to a laugh. Lines that are neither red nor green should be cut, unless they contain essential information. In which case find ways of making them funny.

A sketch can often be like a stage farce in miniature. Don't worry about getting laughs right from the start. The audience needs a moment to understand who these people are, where they are, and the bizarre thing that's about to happen to them. But, once the laughs come, keep up the pace – increase it if possible – right up to the end.

Alan Stafford, writer for Griff Rhys Jones, Punt and Dennis, Rory Bremner, Russ Abbot and many others

SKETCH TRY-OUT

Here's the how the 'Disgusting Chef' sketch turned out. I've named it 'Sourced in the Kitchen'. It's still quite rough but it does give a feel of what the finished sketch could be like.

<u>SOURCED IN THE KITCHEN</u>
A SMART LOOKING RESTAURANT. TWO DINERS (PIERS AND AMANDA) ARE LOOKING AT THE MENUS. THEY ARE APPROACHED BY THE WAITER.

WAITER:	Let me explain our concept, monsieur. Everything on the menu is entirely made from produce sourced solely within our kitchen.
AMANDA:	Mmmm.
PIERS:	Glad I took you here, Mands? It's supposed to be a top place. Well, for starters, I think I'll go for the salade verte épousseté.
WAITER:	Excellent choice, monsieur.
PIERS:	Great! Green salad with a light dusting.
AMANDA:	What's it dusted with?
WAITER:	Dust. From the kitchen. As I said, entirely locally sourced.
PIERS:	And the salade verte?
WAITER:	Mould, monsieur. Again, entirely from the kitchen. And garnished with chef's own croutons: deep fried oven scrapings.
AMANDA:	I think I'll give the starters a miss.
PIERS:	(TO THE WAITER) Women – can't handle concepts. OK – mains it is.
AMANDA:	What's the jus cancrelat en lasagne de pacquet de soupe de jambon?
WAITER:	Ah. The lasagne is made from strips of ham soup packets we found in the larder. Last year's and they've aged beautifully. The jus is made from cockroaches. We're very proud of our cockroaches.
AMANDA:	This is dreadful!
WAITER:	If Madame is upset with the thought of jus of cockroach, that is understandable. Maybe she would prefer live ones. They look beautiful as they scuttle over the plate and of course would be extremely fresh.
PIERS:	It's challenging, but rewarding. Slow food, that's so last year.

WAITER: And if you can't face them right away, we are happy to let you
            put them in a bag and take them home.

A SCREAM IS HEARD FROM THE KITCHEN.

PIERS: I like to hear a chef who expresses himself.

WAITER: He'll be working on his bouillabaisse de sous chef. It is famous.

THE SOUS CHEF DASHES IN, MOANING AND CLUTCHING HIS
EAR. HE EXITS.

WAITER: Chef's very creative. He prepares the dish by swearing at the
            sous chef just as he is lifting the soup. This makes him drop the
            soup, so chef thrusts his head into the bouillabaisse. Please don't
            be shocked, Madame. He ensures he beats him senseless before
            immersing him.

AMANDA: That's barbaric.

PIERS: You're being so Anglo-Saxon. This is something deep within
            their culture.

WAITER: Then chef picks up his cleaver and adds a revolutionary new
            ingredient to the bouillabaisse – ear of teenager. Sourced, of
            course, from our kitchen.

AMANDA: I've had enough. Piers, we're going.

SHE STANDS UP, PUTS ON HER COAT. RELUCTANTLY PIERS GETS
UP TOO.

ENTER CHEF BRANDISHING HIS CLEAVER.

CHEF: What's this? You cannot go yet! It is not permitted!

THE WAITER PULLS A CLEAVER FROM HIS JACKET. HE AND THE
CHEF STAND THREATENINGLY BETWEEN PIERS AND AMANDA
AND THE DOOR.

WAITER: Sorry, Madame. You are not allowed to contravene the ethos of
            this restaurant. You do not fully understand our concept. Let us
            take you both on a tour of the kitchen.

AMANDA: I'm not going through there.

PIERS: I'm afraid she's rather unadventurous.

CHEF: You must come through. It is not an option.

WAITER: It is the only way by which you can fully participate in our
            experience culturelle.

AMANDA: I'd rather die.

THE WAITER AND CHEF MOVE CLOSER TO PIERS AND AMANDA.

CHEF: At last she grasps our concept.

WAITER: It is trés important that you come through.

CHEF: Do you want our 'Sourced in the Kitchen' concept to be a lie when we serve our pièce de résistance to the next customer?

WAITER: Bourguignon de previous diner!

THE CHEF AND WAITER PRESS PIERS AND AMANDA TO THE KITCHEN DOOR.

PIERS: I told you it was a top place, Mands. Everything's fresh!

Ends

SKETCH EXAMPLE

Here's another, more finished sketch from a talented writer, Dave Baker. See how clear the premise is and how well it develops. The comedy is enhanced by the rhythm of the dialogue. It has been formatted for radio.

SECRET SERVICE CUTBACKS

AN OFFICE. M SITS AT THE DESK. ENTER Q

M: Q, come in and sit down.

Q: M, thanks.

M: You know why you're here.

Q: The Privatisation?

M: That's right, Q, it's official. The coalition government have announced the deal – we've been bought out by Waddington's.

Q: Waddington's? The board game people?

M: That's right. They've agreed that we need to make 10% staff cuts. There are 26 of us in the Department . . .

Q: A through to Z.

M: . . . so, that means two, or possibly three, redundancies.

Q: I saw Z outside earlier. He looked pretty upset. I guess that you've gone for the old 'alphabetical order' approach that we used back in 1992?

M: No, not this time. Waddington's are using their own methods.

Q: So, Z's okay then?

M: No, Z's going. But it's not because of alphabetical order.

Q: But he's reliable, he's been here for ages, why Z?

M: Q, we've *all* been here for ages. And it's the secret service, so we're all pretty reliable. No, Waddington's are going to use their 'Scrabble' solution.

Q: Sorry? Did you say 'Scrabble'?

M: Yes. Our redundancy policy is being organised on the basis of which letters get the most points in Scrabble.

Q: And the government have allowed *that*?

M: I'm afraid so. So, it's you and Z.

Q: U and Z?

M: No, U is safe – he's a one-pointer under the scheme. Like E and A. It's you, Q, who'll be going. Although when you're gone, it is true that U will have slightly less to do.

Q: I'll have *nothing* to do.

M: No, U will have less to do. Honestly, sometimes I wonder why we ever assigned single letters as code names for secret service officers. It can be like the Two Ronnies in here sometimes.

Q: So, it's me and Z?

M: Yes. Sorry.

Q: So, M, what am I going to do?

M: You know the form, Q. Z just took my revolver into the library. He is . . . – or should I say he *was* – a good man.

Q: I see. Forty years' dedicated service, and it comes to this?

M: Q, it's the secret service. You know the rules.

Q: OK, M, give me the gun.

M: Sorry, Q – Z has taken my only weapon.

Q: What should I do, then?

M: Well, there's a lead pipe in the kitchen, or you could use the candlestick in the library.

Q: Waddington's! It's just like some kind of game to them!

Ends

Here are Dave's notes on how he wrote the sketch:

· ·

This started out as a straightforward parody – what would James Bond do if he was facing public sector budget cuts? Sketching the idea out, it seemed that the use of initials 'M' and 'Q' for the spymasters gave additional scope for comic misunderstanding. I was toying with things that could happen to M&S or B&Q when the 'Scrabble points' idea came to me. Then it was just a question of finding a few potential laughs.

The confusion between you and 'U', for instance. In fact I thought this single joke had enough legs for a two-minute sketch – especially playing around with misunderstandings about 'Y' and 'why' – but I struggled to find a decent punchline.

The link between Scrabble and Cluedo came from this problem. Once I'd decided this was the way I wanted it to end, I had to reverse-engineer 'Waddington's' into the start of the sketch – the company had taken over MI6, which seemed like an interesting idea. It's actually Hasbro and Mattel who manufacture Cluedo and Scrabble, but Waddington's seemed to work best, so I stuck with that.

TROUBLESHOOTING

'I've written my sketch. It's five pages long, but I can't trim it back any more. Every line seems to be good stuff.'

First check that your sketch is based on one idea and not two or three. If so, ruthlessly cut out the unwanted matter. You probably can trim it further. Get hold of, or copy, the script of a sketch from a well-known show and see how economical the dialogue is and how focused the structure. Several drafts are sometimes necessary to root out unwanted words, duplicated information and overwritten sentences.

SUMMING UP

- Use normal everyday dialogue.
- Make the speech reflect the character.
- Go over the dialogue many times to cut unwanted words.
- Rewrite the sketch several times.

5
WRITING SKETCHES:
THE DIFFERENT MEDIA

Some outlets for sketches pay very well, some not a great deal, many not at all. At this stage of your career don't be too picky. Some non-paying shows such as Newsrevue in London are a worthwhile addition to your CV.

Each medium presents its own set of delights and problems. Your approach to them should subtly vary. But whether you're writing for TV, radio, the stage or the internet, the basic rules of sketch writing are much the same.

WRITING FOR RADIO

Radio is the home of the first British broadcast comedy and remains a highly important breeding ground for new talent. *Goodness Gracious Me* and *The League of Gentlemen* were originally radio shows. There are more new sitcoms and sketch shows on Radio 4 than on all UK TV channels combined. Nowadays, BBC Radio 7 on digital radio regularly broadcasts shows that showcase new comedy writers. Ignore radio at your peril.

As a medium, radio is:

AURAL

Information is given through dialogue and sound effects. You need to get it across clearly and creatively, while ensuring that your characters sound natural. You must identify them unambiguously, with no confusion as to who's speaking. It's more important than ever to have a small number of parts. Make each character sound different. A lot of this can be done by the casting, but you can lend a hand through using different ages, genders, speech patterns, vocabularies, etc.

IMAGINATIVE

A radio audience is more willing than a TV one to travel with you to the other side of the universe – once their expectations have been stoked. Our minds have no limit. A costume and set budget most certainly does.

This means you can:

- Locate the sketch anywhere. A weather station in the Antarctic, an asteroid circling Jupiter or the inside of someone's stomach are equally easy.
- Use non-human characters. Cats, aliens, Greek gods and robots are all in your potential casting pool.
- Move through time. You can jump twenty years on and back at the flick of an eyelid. The actor won't need elaborate ageing makeup and the set won't need changing. However, you still have to inform the audience seamlessly.

WRITER-FRIENDLY

Radio uses simpler technology than TV. Production teams are smaller and the writer becomes a more central part of the process.

DIALOGUE-FRIENDLY

Much more than TV, radio favours the word. This doesn't give the green light to verbosity but your nuanced dialogue can come into its own. With no distracting visuals, a radio audience is highly sensitive to speech.

- *Non-verbal reactions*: a gasp, a sigh or a grunt can convey as much as a sentence. Think how you can use these and don't be afraid to put them in the dialogue, without overdoing it or insulting the actor's intelligence.
- *Silence*: this can convey a huge amount, depending on the context. It will draw us into the character's thoughts and it provides beats. They can add a whole layer to the meaning:

JANET:	Where were you last night, Jim?
JIM:	(PAUSE) At a meeting.
JANET:	You mean, the pub.
JIM:	No, Janet! Darren wanted an urgent word. He . . . (PAUSE) I've been sacked.
	SILENCE

RADIO SCRIPT LAYOUT

See Figures 4 and 5. The characters' names are in the left-hand column with their dialogue on the same line a tab or two to the right. Always insert a colon after the character's name. In the place of camera instructions are sound effects, signified by 'FX'. These are always on a separate line, bold and underlined. Think every situation through in sounds.

These examples are basic templates to get you up and running. If you look up www.bbc.co.uk/writersroom and go to Scripts in the left-hand column you'll find more detailed examples of TV and radio scripts. They will show you everything you need.

WRITING FOR TELEVISION

Everyone wants a bit of TV glamour. Television has given us some of the greatest sketch moments, has the highest profile and pays the best by a long chalk. From Monty Python to Harry Enfield and *Little Britain*, the TV sketch show at its best is one of the glories of British culture. It's also a tough market to crack.

Television as a medium is:

- Visual. When writing for TV, think at every stage what the audience will see. What do your locations, your characters and their actions look like? How many of your verbal jokes could be visual ones?
- Expensive. A TV crew consists of a small crowd of people working on the cameras, the sound, wardrobe, makeup, the set, etc. This all costs a lot of money. It costs even more to use

<u>NAME OF SKETCH</u> by A. Writer

Email address
Phone no. (on
every page)

FX	**CLINKING GLASSES**

1. JACK: Cheers, Jill.

2. JILL: You had no need to say that, Jack. The information that we're in
a pub was carried in the FX line – i.e. sound effects.

FX	**JACK'S MOBILE RINGS. HE PICKS IT UP**

3. JACK: Hello.

4. BEN: (D) Offsketch here. We police quality control in sketch writing.
Look, that clinking glass FX to signify a pub is a bit of a cliché.

5. JACK: I never listen to anyone who starts their dialogue with a (D).

6. BEN: (D) That means "distort". Which is what a voice sounds like on
the other end of the phone.

FX	**PHONE SWITCHED OFF**

7. JACK: This radio writing is really stressful.

GRAMS	**CALMING ANDEAN PIPE MUSIC**

8. JILL: That better? Not only does the BBC have a huge selection of
music recordings called "Grams", it can also read your mind.
And when you want to end the sound, just go:

GRAMS	**OUT**

9. JILL: See?

10. JACK: Thank heavens for that. I hate Andean pipe music. By the way,
my name is Jack, not 10 Jack. I am a man, not a number!

(1)

Figure 4: Radio Layout

NAME OF SKETCH by A. Writer   Email address
                                                Phone no. (on
                                                every page)

1. JILL: The numbers are a rehearsal aid and start over at the top of

                  each page.

2. JACK: Blow that. If I want to cut a speech, I've got to go back up and

                  change all the numbers.

3. JILL: There's special radio format software you can download from

                  the BBC that does it all for you.

4. JACK: Will it write my clichés for me as well?

5. JILL: That's one for Offsketch.

FX   **A CHAIR IS SCRAPED BACK**

6. JILL: Be seeing you, Jack.

7. JACK: Don't go. I'll have to finish the sketch on my own!

GRAMS   **ANDEAN PIPED MUSIC**

8. JILL: (VO) Does that make you feel calmer?

9. JACK: (VO) Not the piped music! And that weird VO in front of my

                  dialogue isn't helping.

10. JILL: (VO) It just means Voiceover, when we talk over a sound.

GRAMS   **OFF**

11. JACK: Thanks. So, I've got to finish the sketch . . . Ah, I know!

FX   **CLINK OF GLASSES**

12, JACK: Cheers, Jill!

13. JILL: Reincorporation. How clever.

ENDS

                        (2)

Figure 5: Radio Layout 2

elaborate sets or move from one location to another. Keep it simple.

- Realistic. This doesn't mean that your comedy can't be way out and surreal. But keep the visual style ordinary and everyday (see the paragraph above). Wacky sets and bizarre costumes can be visually jarring, especially when they've bombarded the viewer for half an hour.

→ NOW TRY THIS

When you're submitting to a TV show, write two or three sketches in the same location. The more everyday it is, the easier it will be to think of a number of ideas. This will improve your chances of having more than one sketch accepted.

TV LAYOUT

New writers can get very nervous about TV layouts but there are no precise rules for presenting your script. The main thing is to ensure that dialogue and action are clearly separated and that you've thought about how it will look. Don't worry about camera instructions, two shots or establishing shots. You job is to present the dialogue and necessary actions and visuals as sparsely as possible. The director and camera crew will look after anything more technical and TV-ish.

Figures 6 and 7 give an example of TV layout. There's a wide left-hand margin for camera instructions; the descriptions of the action are between the dialogue; and there's a separate line for the character's name. It's important that the sketch name, your name and contact details, and the page number are clear on every page. You don't want the reader to pick up your brilliant script and find they can't identify you.

TITLE OF SKETCH (On every page)   email & phone   (1
By A. Writer   on every page

INT: MORNING: THE SPARE ROOM IN A FLAT

> JILL TYPES WHILE JACK PACES. THE DESK IS
>
> COVERED WITH CRUMPLED TISSUES. THE
>
> ROOM LOOKS A MESS.

JACK

A mess? I object to that!

JILL

The section in regular capitals under the bold scene
description describes what the viewer will see.

> JACK WIPES HIS FACE WITH A FRESH TISSUE.

JILL

The action is always laid out separately from the dialogue
and should be described sparingly. Describe the
character's emotion with a brief word in bracketed
capitals. (BRIGHTLY) Just like that! Don't insult the actor's
intelligence by overdoing it.

Figure 6: Television Layout 1

TITLE OF SKETCH (On every page)   email & phone   (2
by A. Writer   on every page.

JILL

Oh, and if you must carry a speech onto a second page,

put in the character's name again.

JACK

I see everything is in a normal typeface and is double-

spaced. So when are you going to let me do the typing?

JACK'S PHONE GOES

JACK

(INTO PHONE) Hello?

BEN

(D) Offsketch here again. You're to use more visual

humour.

JACK THROWS THE COMPUTER OUT OF THE

WINDOW

JACK

Visual enough?

Ends

Figure 7: Television Layout 2

WRITING FOR THE STAGE

Alongside the solo acts in comedy clubs you'll often see duos, trios and quartets of people performing sketches. Most of these acts use their own material, but some of them may well use non-performing writers and are worth approaching if you'd like to write but not perform. If on the other hand you enjoy performing, it could well be worth your while to join up with some friends and act your sketches. This is how *Little Britain* and *The League of Gentlemen* started. If acting isn't your cup of tea, there are stage sketch shows for which you can write. You can find these in the Appendix.

KEEP IT SIMPLE

You'll probably have no budget. Costumes may only go as far as hats. Props and sets are supplied by the audience's imagination. You may be able to make a sound effects CD, but the more complicated it is, the more things can go wrong.

KEEP IT SMALL

A stand up comedy stage may only fit two people if they don't step sideways. So, to show any action much more space-consuming than breathing you'll have to enlist the audience's imagination. You can land on the moon and be chased by alien dinosaurs as you bound across the Tycho Crater, but it will be on the spot. There'll probably only be two or three of you, but you can suggest a big cast if you're adept with hats and voices.

MAKE IT BROAD

A radio comedy listener may be happy to chuckle along as they do the ironing. A live stage crowd needs to laugh aloud frequently. You must go out and grab the audience with big jokes. Clarity is all: belly laughs are vital and subtlety may go unnoticed.

TV and radio shows use music links between sketches: one sketch follows another in the space of a heartbeat. On stage, it takes a second or two to get off and on, to pick up props or simply to change gear. To cover these gaps and maintain the energy, make sure every sketch ends with a big laugh.

PLAY ON THEIR IMAGINATION

Audiences are happy to be led to wherever you can take them, but you must do it boldly. Just as in radio, you can go from the jungle to the deck of HMS *Victory* in the twinkling of an eye.

PUTTING ON YOUR OWN SHOW

Staging a forty-five-minute or hour-long show will involve a lot of hard work, but will be well worth it in terms of experience and building a profile.

WRITING THE MATERIAL

Twenty or twenty-five sketches should be enough. Make sure all your material is able to be staged. Try to give the show a theme and keep it 'of the moment'. Needless to say, finding a partner in the project will help immeasurably.

FIND A SPACE

Does your local pub have an upstairs room? There are plenty of landlords willing to hire out a space very reasonably, or even let you have it for free, grateful for the extra trade. All you need is enough space to seat twenty or thirty people, some chairs and a few extra square feet to act as a stage.

FIND SOME ACTORS

There are thousands of talented and enthusiastic professional actors round the country, most of whom, sadly, at any one time will be out of work. Many of them are eager for experience and may be happy to perform for expenses-only in between other acting jobs, although don't insult their professionalism by assuming this.

Don't use your mates. Enthusiasm is no substitute for training when it comes to timing a line, finding a character or using an accent.

Make friends with your local amateur theatre group. They are also excellent places to get performers and support, and if you get in with them may be prepared to lend equipment such as lights.

Use between four and six actors. If there are fewer, they'll be too stretched. If there are more, a small space can become very crowded.

PLAN THOROUGHLY

Allow about ten rehearsals, spread over about three weeks. Be minute in your planning, from the times you will need each actor to giving them their props in good time. Your main assets as a director will be your knowledge of the material, a thoroughly organized schedule and a friendly, collaborative attitude with the actors. You'll probably be delighted at their contribution.

ADVERTISE

Use Facebook and word of mouth, and print out a simple leaflet. Drop these off at local libraries, pubs and a local comedy club if you have one. You need enough of an audience to raise decent laughs, so don't stretch things too thin by programming more than one or two performances.

LEARN FROM THE EXPERIENCE

After the show you'll have gained some priceless insights into what works and, just as importantly, what doesn't. You'll have found out what actors can bring to a script. You'll see that your best-loved lines don't always get the most laughs. Those which do are often the ones you threw in almost without thought.

Above all, you'll have found out that comedy is a collaborative art form between writer, performer, director and, most importantly, the audience.

MAKING A VIDEO

USING THE INTERNET AS A SHOWCASE

YouTube is the perfect vehicle for sketches. You can make three-minute videos, post them and build a good audience if your video is good and you are internet-savvy. Some of the most-watched videos were filmed very simply with unambitious production values. What matters is that your film is accessible and has immediate appeal.

BE CLEAR ABOUT YOUR AIMS

A warning: 'simply' does not mean 'easily'. A two-minute video is hard to write and hard to film. However good your idea, you won't be able to achieve the quality of a filmed *Armstrong & Miller Show* or *That Mitchell and Webb Look* sketch. A TV producer is unlikely to give you an immediate commission. A video that gets thousands of hits, however, is a useful addition to a CV.

So keep your aims realistic: you want to get your work seen (and see it yourself) and gain some invaluable experience. Place tight limits on your budget and time allocation. Your mantras should be natural light, a small cast, an extremely simple setup, one scene, few camera angles and a close edit. Write sketches with no elaborate visual effects or complicated action.

Perform it yourself: if you have the slightest yen to perform, now is the time to give it an airing. Acting for the camera is largely a matter of being natural and bringing the performance down rather than amplifying it. Think about writing a string of monologues that fit you like a glove and won't need too much 'acting'. Remember that a closeup lens is a wonderful way of revealing quirks and idiosyncrasies.

EQUIPMENT NEEDED

- *Cameras*: you can buy a simple camcorder for well below £50 and a more sophisticated one for something over £100, though the more you pay, the higher the quality of your camera. You don't need expensive lights and paraphernalia. You can shoot a very effective scene using natural light, indoors or outdoors.

- *Editing equipment*: you can make your rough-and-ready video look more professional with some deft editing. There is a variety of free software available, such as Windows Movie Maker, which can be easily downloaded and gives you a wide range of possibilities. You do not need to buy expensive commercial editing equipment.

CREATING ANIMATION

Although the British TV industry has yet to produce a major animated sitcom hit, the internet has created opportunities and easily accessible tools for this genre, which is such a great medium for sketches.

- *Creating a visually striking style*: with the different types of animation available, from drawn animation and stop-go to cut-outs and models, you can, without developed artistic skills, produce a sketch in a distinctive visual format.
- *Building a series*: if you can create an idiosyncratic style, it follows that you can make a series of sketches that have your unique stamp on them.
- *Creating extraordinary characters*: there are no limitations on the appearance of your characters. You can have animals as your protagonists or breathe life into inanimate objects.

TYPES OF ANIMATION

- *Drawn animation*: today there is computer software that will do much of the labour-intensive work of traditional animation. You can draw an image using a pencil tool on to a key frame and create a second image by transferring it to another frame along the timeline and slightly altering it – and so on. You don't need to be a highly proficient artist to produce effective results.

- *Cut-outs*: *South Park* showed the way for those who wanted to use deliberately primitive artwork or who simply couldn't draw. The pilot episode was made traditionally by the stop-motion filming of paper cut-outs; after that the process was computerized. There is software enabling you to create your own two-dimensional figures and place multiple layer backgrounds behind them using key frames. Tweening techniques can be used to build multiple images moving through time. You don't need to draw anything: you can adapt copyright-free images from the internet, or scan in your own.
- *Claymation*: the characters are made from a material such as plasticine formed over a wire skeleton, which is shot frame by frame with slight variations. An illusion of movement is created when it is projected at about twenty-four frames per second. Great care must be taken with the lighting and to maintain continuity. Modelling skills and patience will be in great demand, but the final results can be captivating.

WRITING FOR ANIMATION

- *Go anywhere you like*: just as in radio, you can set your story on the far side of Pluto or in the interior of someone's brain as cheaply and easily as at a bus stop.
- *Use sparse dialogue*: it is impossible to create a full range of lip movements to follow the dialogue. Speeches should be very simple and short.
- *Avoid showing the speaker's face*: it follows that it is easier to show the reactions of the listener to the speech in voiceover. You can show the speaker at a distance, inside a car or the back of their head to minimize views of their face.
- *Using sound*: the use of music and effects are crucial to the success of animation. There are many copyright-free FX websites, making it easy to record and edit sounds. You can simply drag the sound from the library and drop it into the key frame.

GETTING TRAINING

Look in the Appendix for websites offering training in basic animation techniques.

⸱⸱⸱

With animation you can set a sketch wherever you want so you can be as imaginative as you like. Keep the animation simple and try to avoid more complicated things such as characters walking in a realistic way. Always plan your animation before you start or you will find yourself going round in circles.

Richard Woolford, whose animation *The Grave* won the 2013 Dave's Comedy Festival Comedy Short first prize

⸱⸱⸱

Exercise

Now look at the sketch you wrote at the end of the previous chapter. Is it more suited for radio or TV? How would you handle the actions, sounds and speech for each medium? Lay it out for your chosen medium. Now file it. The time may well come when, with a little reworking, you'll be able to sell it.

SUMMING UP

- Radio can be a very imaginative medium but you must convey all your information aurally. It demands a specific layout of the script.
- Television involves tighter budgets and a more visual way of thinking. It also has its own specific layout.
- You can perform your own sketches or stage a sketch show using actors. A live audience means the laughs must be frequent and loud.
- Putting your comedy videos on the internet does not require expensive equipment and can be a useful experience.
- Animation is well suited for sketch comedy and can be done by amateur artists using the right software.

6
WRITING SKETCHES: QUICKIES

WHAT IS A QUICKIE?

Quickies are the very short sketchlets that punctuate sketch shows. On TV they're often entirely visual. Their main function is to add pace and variety to the comedy. A string of sketches of roughly equal length creates a predictable rhythm. It's better to break it up with a few very short pieces, each of which gets a good laugh in its own right.

Here are the main attributes of a quickie:

- Short (thirty seconds roughly);
- One big laugh;
- A dramatic situation;
- Limited number of characters (usually one to four);
- One setting;
- Based on one idea;
- Strong visual impact.

Think of a quickie as a joke that is told using actors and scenery. The whole point is the payoff at the end, but it needs a clear setup, which is then twisted or turned around. If this doesn't lead to a good laugh, you've wasted thirty seconds.

Don't write anything you don't care about just to be 'expedient' – because it will only ever be competent at best. Is it an idea that will strike a real chord with an audience? Who do you think will want to see it? If you have a burning desire to write, then it's more likely to grab our attention.

BBC Writersroom

WRITING QUICKIES

KEEP IT VERY SIMPLE
The fewer characters the better. A quickie rarely takes up more than a page of script: there's no time for dialogue for more than about three people. Keep to one set, preferably something everyday.

MAKE THE SITUATION RECOGNIZABLE
You have no time to set up an elaborate situation: the audience have to grasp what is going on instantaneously. Settings like restaurants, bus stops and doctor's surgeries are immediately recognizable. Spoofs of well-known movie scenes come into their own here, as long as they are kept simple.

ONE BIG LAUGH
A quickie has to earn its keep. A string of funny-ish gags won't do the trick. The one laugh needs to be a really good one.

ESTABLISH THE ACTION IMMEDIATELY
You can set up a sketch within a few lines but you must establish a quickie in the first second. Subtle characterization or elaborate setups become problematic. Simple archetypal situations work best. For example: we see the corridor in a block of flats. A man has answered the door to a woman. She announces herself as a new neighbour and asks to borrow a cup of sugar. The man goes inside and comes out with a couple of full packets. The woman, delighted at this generosity, leaves with the sugar. The man beckons inside to his partner who carries a sack: they have been burgling the flat.

THINK VISUALLY
Many quickies have no dialogue. One *Alas Smith & Jones* quickie established an Asian food counter with a sign saying, 'All you can eat for £5.00.' A man spooned a mountain of food on to his plate. He took it next door to another food buffet. He spooned the food

into these containers: it was his own counter. Above we saw a sign saying, 'All you can eat for £10.00.'

GETTING IDEAS FOR QUICKIES

You get ideas for quickies in just the same way as for sketches. Use whichever way works best for you: choose a subject, break it down into different topics and subtopics, and turn the raw material into comedy ideas.

PLAY WITH THE IDEA

Could the neighbour quickie be improved? Maybe the new neighbour has some luggage with her and is asking the man to look out for her flat as she's going away for a week. He expresses delight and, as the woman goes away, beckons his partner-in-crime to tell him her flat is their next job. Which idea is better? I'm not sure. But by some lateral thinking I've given myself two possibilities from one setup.

Sometimes a bit of research produces gold. Monty Python's brilliant Millionaire sketch ('Luxury!') can be found in the works of Stephen Leacock. Find out how the masters got laughs.

Peter Vincent

QUICKIE EXAMPLE

Although very compressed, a quickie still has a setup, a build and a payoff. The payoff is the most important moment but the other two need to be in place, just as in a sketch. You can build a story in a few seconds. Let's look at the quickie below.

<u>INT: DAY. A WOMAN'S BEDROOM</u>
WE SEE TOM AND KATY IN TWO SHOT.
KATY HAS BEEN CRYING.

TOM

I'm terribly, terribly sorry about last night, Katy. What I did was unforgivable.

KATY

You and your sweet talk, Tom. How do I know you mean it this time?

TOM HOLDS UP A LITTLE FLUFFY TOY
SQUIRREL WITH A RIBBON ROUND IT AND A NOTE ATTACHED.

TOM

I got you this. I know how you love squirrels. He's called Mr Tufty.

HE HOLDS UP MR TUFTY AND IN A GENTLE SQUIRRELLY VOICE
READS THE NOTE.

TOM

'Tom is truly sorry about last night, believe me. Please forgive him.'

HE GIVES MR TUFTY TO KATY.

TOM

He's for you.

KATY

Oh, he's lovely . . . you really won't ever do it again, Tom? I . . . I just couldn't
stand it . . .

TOM

Never, ever. Believe me.

KATY CUDDLES MR TUFTY. SHE SMILES AT TOM AND HOLDS HIS
HAND.

THE CAMERA CUTS BACK. KATY PUTS MR TUFTY ON A SHELF. THE
WHOLE SHELF IS FULL OF TOY SQUIRRELS, LARGE AND SMALL,
ALL WITH RIBBONS TIED ROUND WITH A NOTE ATTACHED.

Ends

There is an emotional build. Before the visual payoff we see Tom's
apology, the offer of the squirrel and Katy's acceptance. It was
important that Tom and his present are charming and that the
characters' emotions are real and strong.

Exercise

Write a quickie. Give it a visual payoff.

→ NOW TRY THIS

Work backwards from the payoff to the setup. I'm looking at my ancient Anglepoise lamp. It looks rather like a hair dryer. Imagine a woman sitting under it. Why would she be there? What could have happened? That could be the build-up. I don't know what it could be, but there may be a quickie in it.

TROUBLESHOOTING

'I can't decide which of my ideas are suitable for quickies and which would be best for a sketch.'

If you see the situation running on with at least three good laughs then you probably have a sketch idea. If you can't think of an immediate ending but think the idea is funny, then, again, it's probably a sketch (and you need to think of an ending!). If the payoff comes to you immediately and it's strong, it's probably a quickie.

'I've been staring at my ideagram for half an hour and haven't thought of a single funny idea.'

Give yourself a break. Then try to use a different method or another sense. For example, if you've been using a verbal ideagram, look at some pictures. Or next time you're out and about in a public space spend five minutes looking and listening. To what could your observations be compared? Can you place them in another context? How could they be turned upside down?

SUMMING UP

- Quickies are short – thirty seconds on average.
- They involve a beginning, a middle and an end, just like a sketch but much more compressed.
- They involve one big laugh.
- The humour tends to be visual.
- They are conceived in much the same way as sketches.

7
WRITING SKETCHES: CHARACTER SKETCHES

Character sketches have played a huge role in British comedy, from *The Dick Emery Show* through to *The Fast Show*, *Little Britain* and *The Armstrong & Miller Show*. They often make big stars of the performers and help the writers develop strong careers. They can be just as funny as the cerebral comedy of Monty Python or *Big Train* and are even more quotable. But the comedy comes from another place altogether from idea sketches and entails a very different writing process.

WRITING CHARACTER COMEDY

The audience aren't laughing at an absurd concept but at the foibles of someone they've come to recognize and maybe even love. The focus is entirely on the character. Who's Vicky Pollard in *Little Britain* going to brush up against? How's she going to react? When's she going to come out with her catchphrase? She's at the centre of everything.

The writer must create a person who's larger than life and recognizable, and whose reactions we can enjoy in scenario after scenario. You're not coming up with numerous ideas for disconnected sketches but building an unforgettable character who returns time and time again to make us laugh.

Over a two-minute period, you can't put them through what screenwriting gurus call a character arc. We see the same behaviour again and again. There's no change: if there was, the audience would feel betrayed. The character must be not only vivid but consistently funny over many scenes.

A DIFFERENT WRITING APPROACH

Rather than a spate of quirky ideas, you're building something that can be maintained over at least four sketches. Before writing any dialogue you need to do some road-testing to see whether your character has mileage.

CHARACTER COMES FIRST

Your centrepiece has to be funny, distinctive and defined enough to keep the audience enthralled time and time again. If there's a flaw in their design, they will break down after a couple of sketches.

YOU'RE WRITING A SERIES

Individual sketches matter less than the overall impact of the character. If your character only delivers you one sketch, fine, but it's a stand-alone idea.

ESSENTIALS OF A SKETCH CHARACTER

THEY HAVE THE ONE OVERRIDING CHARACTERISTIC

Sketch characters are cartoons. They tend to be highly exaggerated and present the same trait in every sketch. In real life they may also be kind to animals or know how to cook a great lasagne but in a sketch we never find this out. You need to isolate one trait and cut out everything else. It follows that this one unique quality needs to be compelling, idiosyncratic and, of course, very funny.

- *The characteristic is specific*: it may even be quite a subtle detail. A character whose single quality is something very generalized usually won't work. For example, I may have an idea for a character who simply is highly ingratiating. In every sketch he sidles up to people and fawns on them. Without further exploration this highly obsequious behaviour won't make him come across as an individual and we'll quickly lose patience with him. We need to look at the obsequiousness more closely.

- *The characteristic springs from a motive*: if our man is ambitious and desperate to network his obsequiousness begins to make sense. Perhaps he sees every encounter as an opportunity to advance himself. By putting him in the most inappropriate situations we could begin to create some comedy. So this is our character: he treats everyone he meets as someone who might give him a job.

THEY ARE INSTANTLY RECOGNIZABLE

- *In appearance*: sketch characters are abnormal people. Their behaviour can be extreme and there is often something distinctive or even outrageous about their appearance. So when dreaming up your character ask yourself early on about their physique and dress.
- *In speech*: exaggerate abnormalities in the way they talk. Let them express themselves in their own inimitable vocabulary and sentence structure. Well-chosen words, jargon and slang are a godsend in creating characters.
- *Through catchphrases*: not every sketch character has their own catchphrase, but they can help define them. Think of Vicky Pollard and her 'Yeah but no but . . .' or Harry Enfield's irritating know-all with his hectoring 'You don't wanna to do it like that!' This character was actually named 'Mr Don't Wanna Do It Like That!' Both catchphrases spring directly from the character. They are not funny in themselves but in the mouth of the character they are hilarious.

THEY RUN IN A SERIES OF SKETCHES

We laugh as we get to know their foibles in scenario after scenario. One sketch wouldn't work: they need time to bed in. A series of four sketches is a minimum for one of these characters: a well-created one will 'have legs' for many more.

THEY GO THROUGH THE SAME MOTIONS

They perform an invariable pattern of behaviour in every situation. This pattern can be quite simple or have a more involved sequence. Vicky Pollard is challenged in the middle of a minor misdemeanour, answers back rudely, is challenged again, tries to make excuses as she goes into her 'Yeah, but no but . . .' routine, and finally slips into an incomprehensible rant in which she blames all her mates.

Let's have a look at our networker man (I see him as male). He could approach someone at a gathering, effusively introduce himself and ask what the other person does. Whatever the answer he replies, 'That must be fantastically interesting!' and tries to present himself as someone with just the right skill-set for that job. Naturally he will always be rebuffed. I see him responding sulkily, with an 'I didn't want your lousy job anyway' attitude.

Don't underestimate the contribution your performers can make to your sketch. If you write interesting quirky characters, your cast will enjoy performing them and bring them alive in ways you never imagined.

Alan Stafford

Exercise
Look at three sketches involving well-known sketch characters on DVD or the internet. Ask yourself, 'What is their overriding characteristic?' Then ask yourself, 'What is their invariable pattern of behaviour?'

LOCATING YOUR SKETCH CHARACTER
Just as with everyone else, we see sketch characters through their reactions to other people and to their environment. So against whom shall we pit our characters and where shall we place them?

FINDING YOUR SUPPORTING CAST

- *People who exacerbate their trait*: other people will push, goad or tempt your character towards the behaviour that we find so enjoyable. We only see one side of their personality, so they will usually brush up against the same kind of person: those who set them off.

    Vicky Pollard is always being confronted by authority figures: store detectives, doctors, swimming pool attendants. They're people she meets in the course of her daily life who set off one of her bolshy/defensive rants. Harry Enfield's Mr Don't Wanna Do It Like That! only meets people who are trying to do some simple task, which he insists on correcting.

    My networking man needs to brush up against people in inappropriate situations that he misreads as opportunities. I see them generally as too polite to give him an instant brush-off. This gives him a chance to get into his fawning mode.

- *Use the same or different characters in each sketch*: sometimes your character will always bump up against the same people, as long as you can find a range of situations for them. Occasionally two main characters, such as Armstrong and Miller's teenage-talking Spitfire pilots, only need to react to each other. Mostly you'll find it's best to pit them against a range of people. There are no rules – just pick the supporting cast most likely to maximize the comedy.

CHOOSING YOUR LOCATIONS

Your setting may pick itself. Just ask where your character goes through their routine – and stick to it.

- *The same or different settings?* This will depend on your character's lifestyle. Vicky Pollard wanders the streets so her sketches happen all over town. *The Fast Show*'s Rowley Birkin, whom we only see when very drunk, is always in his club, drink in hand, before the fire. Networking man needs to wander. I will take him anywhere, outdoors or indoors, wherever he mistakenly spots an opportunity.

CREATING YOUR CHARACTER

You're drawing a cartoon, not a rounded lifelike painting. Your picture will be two-dimensional, done with broad strokes, with one trait accentuated until the others become insignificant or are even eliminated altogether.

This doesn't mean that your portrait is un-lifelike. The great sketch characters come across as very vivid and real people, albeit ones from whom we'd probably run a mile. Their emotions and desires should be strong and human. The audience needs to connect with them emotionally or they simply won't stick with them.

FINDING YOUR CHARACTER

You can find them anywhere – at work, on the train, in the pub, on TV, in magazines – or they might spring up entirely in your head. It could be a combination of these. It's probably best to keep away from family and close friends: if we know someone too well it's hard to isolate a characteristic. Besides, your partner may not be too pleased to discover they were the model for the maniac you've created.

- *Go for a detail*: look around you with your antennae quivering for human quirks. Be alert for turns of phrase or tics which you can exaggerate. Allow characters to drift through your head. When someone interesting wafts into view, focus on what is promising about them. Isolate their quirk, which may only be a tiny part of their overall personality. The real person will probably be unrecognizable from your finished creation.

- *Revolve them in your head*: play them through in your imagination. If they don't stay in focus, audition someone else. When a character does stick around, complete this questionnaire on them.

HOW TO WRITE A SKETCH CHARACTER
Ask yourself:

- What is their overriding character attribute that you want to exaggerate?
- What is the invariable pattern of behaviour that springs out of this attribute?
- What do they sound like?
- What do they look like?
- What is their name?
- What is their age?
- What is their gender?
- What is their occupation?
- With whom do they clash?

Answer the questions in any order you like, but answer all of them. Write the answers down and be ready to change things. At this stage it's all work in progress.

> **→ NOW TRY THIS**
> Write down a few lines of your character's speech and read them back out to yourself. Don't worry if you're not an actor – this is not a performance. Now stand up and walk around doing the speech, trying to find the emotions and body language. Try improvising a line or two. Do you get any insight into the character? Do you find yourself coming up with phrases that could be used?

> **Exercise**
> Think up a character and complete the questions on them. Visualize the character for a few minutes with the sharper focus you have given them. Put them in their typical situation. How do they behave and speak? Jot down anything promising.

Honesty first and last. The worst comedy writing invents both a voice and fabricates scenarios that the inexperienced writer thinks might deliver the gags. This is fatal, a bit like a guy faking an orgasm . . . Just write in your own voice about how you and only you see the dysfunctional, the crazy and the funny under the surface of things.

Brent Quinn, writer and Head of Film at
AFDA Film School, South Africa

SKETCH TRY-OUT

Let's do the questionnaire with the networking man.

- *Overriding character attribute*: pushily ingratiating. I see him brazenly approaching people and butting into conversations, at the same time pathetically keen to impress them.
- *Invariable pattern of behaviour*: this can be refined as I go on, but he will buttonhole an unwilling stranger and try to sell himself to them as someone who is great at what they do. He'll try to foist his card on them and, when rebuffed, turn on them.
- *Sounds like*: I see him talking fast and over-enthusiastically. A possible catchphrase is 'Wow! That must be fantastically interesting!' when the other person divulges what they do.
- *Looks like*: always in smart casual suit and open shirt. I see him as being quite lean, with slightly tousled hair.
- *Name*: I'll call him Ned
- *Age*: thirty-five to forty-ish.

- *Occupation*: he's probably a minor clerk in a large corporation, sorry for himself for being underemployed.
- *With whom does he clash?* People whom he sees as good networking fodder but without a job to offer.

NOW TURN IT INTO A SERIES

Think of three scenarios for the character that involve questions 1 and 2 in 'How to write a sketch character'. I'll do this for Ned the Networker (as I'll call him).

- *Sketch 1*: He approaches people at a funeral. 'Mourner? That must be fantastically interesting!' He is rebuffed and accuses them of paying more attention to the deceased than to him. He is removed.
- *Sketch 2*: He's at a party talking to a woman whom he vaguely recognizes. It turns out she's his wife. He tries to sell himself to her, but the only jobs she has going are the washing up and paying the bills.
- *Sketch 3*: He has been captured by jihadis in the desert and tries to network with them.

Here's sketch two:

NED THE NETWORKER SKETCH 2 (PARTY)
A PARTY. DRINK IN HAND, NED IS TALKING TO A WOMAN.

NED:	Hi! Nice do, this! Great to meet you. The name's Quigley. Ned Quigley. Networking, getting on, making contacts, that's me! Didn't catch your name.
MARCIA:	Marcia.
NED:	Marcia . . . sure I know you from somewhere . . .
MARCIA:	I'm your wife.
NED:	Of course! Ha! My wife, wow, that must be fantastically interesting.
MARCIA:	Mmmm, I'm not so . . .
NED:	But that's amazing, we're in the same line of business! What an opportunity, let's exchange cards. I'm a good team player and I get things done.

MARCIA:	Good. How about the washing up afterwards?
NED:	. . . and I'm known for my high-level financial expertise.
MARCIA:	In that case, pay the gas bill.
NED:	So. Huh. I see. I see. It's a shut-door policy, no outsiders, I get it. Exclude the talent. Shoot down the high-flyers. No wonder this country's on its uppers.
MARCIA:	I don't have a job to give you, Ned.
NED:	No job. Huh. That's what they all say. Typical. The Old Boy network. The cosy clique, secret handshake Establishment. Keep out the little man. You're all blind to my real ability.
MARCIA:	And what would that be?
NED:	Can't you see, you cretin? MY PEOPLE SKILLS!!!

Ends

Exercise

Think up three possible sketch situations for your character and write a few lines summarizing each sketch. Now write out one of the sketches in full.

TROUBLESHOOTING

'I've got a character based on someone I know. Although they're hilarious in real life, the sketch ideas seem flabby and just aren't funny.'

Try extrapolating the character from their context. For example, you know a woman at work who obsesses about her cats. In real life most of her everyday interactions will be banal. So lose everything about her apart from her cat obsession. How would she behave on a blind date? At a job interview? Being cross-examined in court? Don't be afraid to exaggerate.

'OK, I've done as you said. What I have now is some very thin, repetitive stories that are far-out but have no impact.'

Find her motive for talking about cats. Maybe she's in a constant state of anxiety about leaving the cats at home and wants to excuse herself from every situation so she can rush back and put out the milk. This immediately sets up conflict between her and the other person. Play various emotions and motives through in your mind. If the character still doesn't work, go and find another.

SUMMING UP

- The comedy in a character sketch focuses on one, unchanging character.
- Character sketches come in a series.
- We see just one aspect of the character – but it needs to be memorable.
- The character will go through an invariable routine.
- They are thrust into a series of situations that exacerbate this characteristic.
- They may or may not use the same supporting cast and setting in each sketch.

8
WRITING SKETCHES: SUBMITTING YOUR WORK

SUBMITTING IN VOLUME
No one will be impressed if you only send in one sketch at a time. Producers are more interested in a writer who can produce a consistent flow of good material than a temperamental genius who writes one masterpiece.

SKETCHES AND QUICKIES
Send in about six to eight in a batch. Any more may make the overworked reader's eyes glaze over. Fewer could look as if you've run out of ideas.

ONE-LINERS FOR RADIO
Ten to twenty is a good number, laid out clearly on one sheet and numbered so the director can refer to them.

MULTIPLE BATCHES
Don't be discouraged if you get no response from your first couple of batches. You'll probably need to send several submissions before you're noticed. If you submit three batches in as many weeks, you start to look serious about your writing and they may begin to take notice.

RINGING IN
If you're submitting to an advertised new writers' showcase don't call up to check your sketches have been received. The director and readers will probably be unavailable, and anyway won't be grateful to people who use up their valuable time. I had success phoning the directors of one show and placing my sketches with them, but they

were featuring few non-commissioned writers and they were less inundated.

RESEARCHING THE SHOW

Make sure your sketches are what they are asking for. Readers for sketch shows grow weary of tossing aside ideas for sitcoms. TV scripts are sent to radio programmes, and shows with a female cast receive sketches featuring three men and a dog. No director gives these a glance.

LISTEN TO THE SHOW

This is essential. The playback facility on the BBC website makes it much easier to research radio shows. If possible, hear two or three previous episodes. Ask yourself:

- What is the style? Broad, grainy, surreal? Does the comedy depend on gags or subtle observation? Does it use historical themes or is it entirely present day?
- What length are the sketches?
- Does the show use quickies, either visual or in the form of one-line gags?
- If it's a topical show, are impressionists used?
- Make a list of all the sketches and their subject matter. This will give you an idea of the ground covered.

READ THE WRITERS' GUIDELINES

The BBC publishes them on the Writersroom page when the show is announced. Study them carefully. If you miss sentences such as 'We're looking for observations of contemporary life, not edgy satire', you could waste hours of your time.

CHECK THE CREDITS

If there are more than five or six writers on the end credits, and especially if there's an announcement 'Additional material by . . .', then the chances are that this is a show which accepts submissions from non-commissioned writers.

→ NOW TRY THIS

Listen to a recording of the show on BBC iPlayer or on CD or DVD. Using the stop/start button, copy out a typical sketch word for word. This will give you a real sense of how the words feel and how it was written.

PRESENTING YOUR MATERIAL

- Use the correct layout.
- Submit six to eight sketches at a time.
- Always present each sketch on a different page. Make sure the numbering begins anew with each sketch if you're sending them in the same file.
- Use one side of the paper only, double-spaced with pages numbered.
- Add a very brief covering note or letter. Don't send in a CV or detailed biography. The reader is not interested in your hilarious article in your school mag. But if you've had sketches on other programmes, or staged your own, do mention this.
- Place your best sketch on the top to make a favourable impression.

SUBMITTING TO TOPICAL SHOWS

There's a good chance that you'll cut your teeth on these shows, so it's worth establishing a modus operandi with them.

FIND A WEEKLY RHYTHM

There's normally a weekly deadline, for example 6 p.m. on Wednesday for a recording on Friday. Organize your schedule: read the papers from Friday onwards and jot down ideas. Spend as much time as you can from Tuesday afternoon to early Wednesday evening writing and rewriting the sketches/jokes before posting them in. Then, start all over again . . .

WHAT KIND OF NEWS?

Some shows deal with the weighty issues of the week, others with frothier stories. They may hand the big issues to the commissioned writers and the smaller stories to the non-commissioned.

WHAT'S THE STYLE?

* *Length of sketches*: some shows consist mainly of very short quickies and one-liners, others sprinkle one-liners between longer sketches.
* *Impressions or not?* A series that uses impressionists will feature sketches about well-known figures, so study the speech patterns of political leaders and celebs. Listen to recordings of the impressionists for a feel of the voices they do and the characters they seem to relish playing.
* *Form of the sketches*: do they consist of lots of broad gags, conversations between ordinary people, spoofs of interviews and TV shows or a run of scattergun quickies? Knowledge is power.

WEB TIPS

For more information and tips on writing sketches, go to www.tonykirwood.co.uk/index.php/script-writing

TROUBLESHOOTING

'I've religiously sent in material every week for the last two series of the show and I've heard nothing.'

Take another look at the writers' guidelines. Maybe you've overlooked something vital. Have you been posting to the right person? Look at your material in the cold light of day. Ask yourself honestly if it was funny or tight enough. If not, don't get depressed. Work to make it funnier and tighter. Just keep trying. Many people don't make their first sale until after months of submitting. Only give up when you're absolutely sure this isn't the show for you. See your work as very useful writing practice and look around for an outlet that suits your talents better.

SUMMING UP
- Research the show thoroughly before submitting.
- Submit six to eight sketches or up to twenty jokes.
- When submitting to topical shows, get into a weekly rhythm of reading the news, writing the material and hitting the deadline.

9
WRITING JOKES: GETTING IDEAS FOR JOKES

Jokes are everywhere. They're part of the social currency of life. People who are good at telling them become popular. Politicians are keen to use them: their messages are much more palatable when peppered with a few good one-liners.

So there's a demand for gags and one-liners. Topical comedy shows eat up jokes about the week's news, TV panel shows use them, musicians and presenters can be desperate for them, you see them on greetings cards, in magazines and, of course, Christmas crackers.

> The best way to have a good idea is to have lots of ideas.
>
> Linus Pauling, winner of two Nobel Prizes

MOST JOKES ARE WRITTEN
A good joke appears to come off the cuff. It thrives on informality and spontaneity. Some people are able to throw them into a conversation at the drop of a hat. However, nearly all the comedians and show presenters who seem to come out with a flow of spontaneous hilarity have spent hours rehearsing. Their skill is to make lines that have been sweated over for hours sound as if they have been made up on the spot. Most of the sweating will have been done by you, the writer.

COMEDY WRITING SKILLS ARE TRANSFERABLE
Your new-found sketch-writing skills will stand you in good stead when writing one-liners. You're now able to brainstorm a wide range

of material and twist it into workable comic ideas. You'll have picked up a thing or two about structure. You'll have learnt how to strip back everything to one central idea. You now know how to be concise. All of these are essential in writing jokes. You have a head start already.

STRUCTURING A JOKE

The classic structure of a joke is:

SETUP   ————————>   PUNCHLINE

It's really a very short story with two acts. The first act, the setup, introduces the idea and gives the audience the picture. It sets up an expectation. The second act, the punchline, subverts the idea. It turns it on its head, twists it around in some way. There's a surprise.

SETUP ————————>	PUNCHLINE
'I asked my boss for a date. She said "Yes."'	'She gave me a month's notice.'
(EXPECTATION)	(SURPRISE)
'Nice bunch of kids on our estate. They stand outside the school gates helping each other with their homework.'	'Dividing seven mobile phones by five'

In both jokes the punchline takes you to a completely different place from the setup. Instead of a romantic date, the boss sacks me. The decent kids turn out to be muggers. As you see, there is a definite 'beat' to a joke. If you can get the 'setup–punchline' rhythm going inside your head, it'll really help you think them up.

How do you compose a joke? Can you come up with these glowing comedy nuggets to order? You can, and one way of doing this is by the good old method of the ideagram.

INSPIRATION FOR JOKES

The wider your field of possible material, the more chance you have of creating laughs. Just as you did with your ideagram in Chapter 2, you can pick a theme that's ripe for comedy, break it down into topics and then see if you can twist the topics into jokes.

For practice, we can start a completely new ideagram. Let's make it on something with which we cope on a daily basis: train travel. Figure 8 shows the results of a few minutes' work.

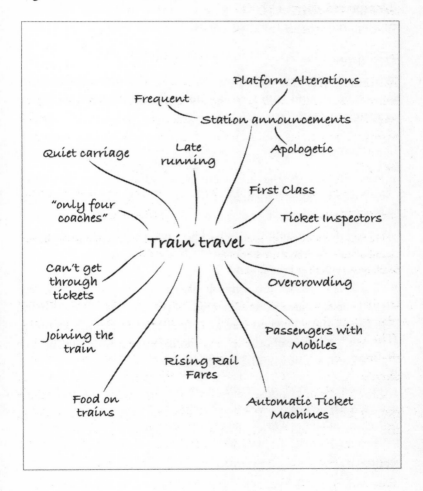

Figure 8

USING JUXTAPOSITIONS

Look round the topics and see if you can combine one with something else, as you did with sketches. Let's try automatic ticket machines. They're rather robotic, like the talking machines at supermarket checkouts. If it could speak, what would it say? 'Unexpected object in bagging area?' 'Insert your card?' Nothing's coming, but at least my brain's starting to tick over.

KEEP TRYING

When fishing for jokes, don't expect one to snap immediately. Keep on swishing round with your line and tell yourself there are plenty of them out there.

USING WORDPLAY

- *Puns*: in a sketch, they can seem crass and cheap, but they work very well in jokes, which, after all, are a verbal form. Look round the topics and see if you can get ideas for playing with words. Let's look at 'Joining the train'. How about: 'We joined the train at Crewe. It was a sweat hooking the engine up, but it was the only way we could get moving.'
- *Figures of speech*: the English language is rich in everyday expressions, proverbs and metaphors that are ripe for wordplay. Jo Brand said, 'The best way to a man's heart is through his breast pocket.' A common cliché is made to mean something utterly different from its original intention.

Let's look at 'Food on trains'. Can we can connect it with an everyday saying? What about 'When in Rome'

'I moaned to my wife I couldn't get served on the train. She said, "When in Rome." I tried, but the buffet attendant didn't speak Latin.'

USING REVERSAL

Can you turn anything on the mind map on its head or inside out? We could try changing the quiet carriage into a noisy carriage, but to me that's a bit tired. Nothing else is coming up at the moment, but that's fine. We can try later on or use another ideagram.

USING EXAGGERATION

That good old warhorse exaggeration can come to your aid with jokes. What would happen if your topic was blown up to absurd proportions? Let's get back to 'food on trains'. It's not always the freshest. What about the sandwiches?

'I'm not saying the sandwich had gone curly – but I was able to hang my coat on it for the rest of the journey'.

COMBINE TECHNIQUES

Jokes are often written using more than one technique. Looking round, I see 'overcrowding'. Let's mix exaggeration with juxtaposition. Imagine a packed carriage crammed like a mosh pit at a rock concert.

'The trains on our line are getting really packed. They're training ticket inspectors in crowd surfing.'

→ NOW TRY THIS

I once overheard some ten-year-old boys competing with each other with cruel but occasionally funny jokes about each other's mother. The form they took was 'Your mother is so ugly that . . .' This is pure exaggeration comedy. Use the same phrasing to help you dream up jokes. You'll almost certainly have to rephrase them with better wording later on.

NOW BREAK THE TOPIC INTO SUBTOPICS

The more detail you find by breaking down your topics the more chance you will give yourself to write jokes. Let's see what we can do with the "Food on trains' topic – see Figure 9. Let's join the buffet topic with celebrity chefs. What would happen if a TV chef was working in the buffet? Imagine Jamie Oliver in the kitchen. He'd fill it with unemployed young people he was trying to train. I can't think of anything particularly funny to do with that. What about Jamie's famous thirty-minute meals?

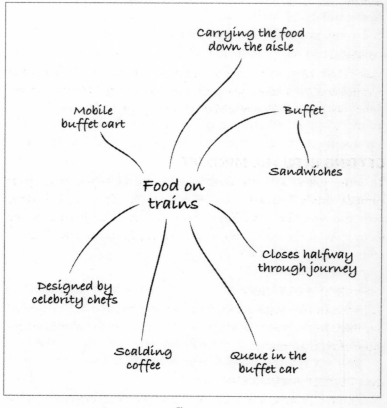

Figure 9

'Jamie Oliver's designed the catering for the London to Brighton service. There'll be just time to do his thirty-minute meals. But after a couple of delays, Jamie's turned them into three-hour meals.'

What if they put another chef in charge?

'Gordon Ramsay's doing the catering. You can hear the swearing right on cue. Every time there's a "we apologize for the delay . . ."'

'Gordon Ramsay's training them in doing the starters. The sous chef stands by, and Gordon tosses the salad.'

These are just initial workings. If you keep on going, you can probably do better.

Exercise

Look at ten jokes from a variety of sources: the internet, joke books and comedians. Ask yourself how each joke is constructed. What technique was used or were a variety brought into play?

GETTING INTO THE MINDSET

To write jokes, as with sketches and quickies, you need your comedy brain turned on. When you're tired and listless, your thoughts feel flat. Your ideagram seems as barren as the mountains of the moon. How can you get into a creative state of mind?

THE JOKES ARE OUT THERE

Tell yourself that jokes are discovered rather than made. They're all out there in the pond, waiting for your hook. Patience finds them more often than genius.

DON'T EXPECT BRILLIANCE RIGHT AWAY

Your aim is to write a number of jokes that work. Brilliance is the icing on the cake.

JUST HAVE A GO

The simple act of looking at a topic and playing games with it will start to crank up your brain. Think of your mind as like an engine. Once it starts to rev, it will pick up speed and the ideas will begin to come. Cut out your internal voice telling you 'it's not funny' and start to jot things down. Something funny will happen.

PRACTISE, PRACTISE, PRACTISE

As with everything else, the more you try to write jokes, the better you get at it. It's like learning any craft, albeit with your mind as your tool. So keep it sharp, and get into the habit of thinking 'Setup–punchline' and how you can twist something so it goes from the first to the second with that delicious gust of surprise.

GOOD IDEAS OFTEN COME AFTER BAD ONES

You can spend half an hour poring over your ideagram and come out with nothing that seems to be any good. The time hasn't been wasted, however. First of all, you've got your mind working. You're in the zone. You've built up more joke possibilities. Sometimes by substituting one image for another or turning the idea upside down, yesterday's clunky non-gag could become something that works.

HONING YOUR JOKES

Getting the idea for a joke, however, is often only half the story. To mould it into words and phrasing that actually make people laugh will take a little more work. Just as with sketches you need to keep your eye on what you've trying to say, on where the comedy lies and on saying it in as few words as possible.

MAKING THE SETUP CLEAR

If the audience don't get the lead-in, they won't get the joke. It has to be immediately understandable and to flow logically into the punchline. Let's have a look at one of the jokes on which we started to work above:

'I moaned to my wife I couldn't get served on the train. She said, "When in Rome." I tried, but the buffet attendant didn't speak Latin.'

At the moment, although we can see there's a joke there, it doesn't really work. 'When in Rome' doesn't fit very well with a buffet-car queue, at least not in any way I can think of. How about changing the situation? How about pubs?

'I went into a rough pub with my wife. Everyone was pushing hard at the bar and I couldn't get the barman's attention. So my wife said, "When in Rome." I tried, but the barman didn't speak Latin.'

It makes more sense but is very clumsy and wordy. By the time we've waded through to the punchline, the audience will have fallen asleep. Hoping she won't mind, I'll cut out my wife.

'I went into a rough pub. Everyone was pushing and I couldn't get the barman to serve me. So I thought, "When in Rome." Didn't work. He couldn't speak Latin.'

If you want to succeed, increase your rate of failure.

Tom Watson, founder of IBM

KEEPING IT CONCISE

- *Cut out unnecessary words*: 'Brevity is the soul of wit,' wrote Shakespeare, in itself a pretty concise statement. Too many words can smother a joke. The more words there are, the harder it is to pinpoint the funny part of the line. A string of pompous words seemed to suit Victorian humour but today we just find it irritating. When you hit upon a joke, you may have had a great idea, but the phrasing is still likely to be clumsy. It's only by rewriting, several times over, that you'll find the best wording. Can we shorten the pub joke?

'In my pub, you've got to fight your way to the bar. When in Rome, eh? Doesn't work. No one speaks Latin.'

• *Use conversational language*: phrase the joke in everyday speech and you will communicate better. Here's another gag, still on the theme of living in a rough area:

'The estate I live on is a really rough one. It's so rough that British Airways had to redirect their plane routes.'

It's OK, but there are too many words and it doesn't trip off the tongue very easily. It lacks the conversational rhythm of good standup material.

'I'm not saying my estate's rough . . . but they did redirect the plane routes.'

From twenty-two words to thirteen. It made the difference between no laugh and a laugh.

PUTTING THE LAUGH AT THE END

Laughs have been lost because the funny part of a joke came in the middle of a sentence. For example, this deaf-dating joke could be improved:

'I've stopped blind-dating men. I now do deaf dating.

It means I don't have to listen to the idiots.'

How about the following?

'I've stopped blind-dating men. I now do deaf dating.

It's great. I don't have to listen!'

The joke is shorter, which can only be good. 'Idiots' at first seemed to be important to the meaning of the joke, but you can do without it, especially if the performer gives the right feeling to the line. The word that should get the laugh is 'listen'.

FINDING FUNNY WORDS

Words with plenty of hard 'k's, 'c's, 'p's and 'g's tend to be funnier. 'Haddock' is definitely funnier than 'fish'. 'Cake' is funnier than 'gateau', 'Macaroni' may be longer than 'penne', but is better for comedy. These hard consonants have more impact and are more audible. Interestingly, they also seem to work better when written. Maybe it's because we unconsciously pronounce words to ourselves when reading jokes (although this hasn't been proven yet).

> **→ NOW TRY THIS**
> Use a simple sentence as your setup and see if you can twist it into a punchline. Try 'The early bird catches the worm.' Can you find a payoff that works with it?

Exercise

Write ten jokes within half an hour, using any technique. Don't worry too much about the quality – just make sure they have a setup and punchline. See which ones could work. File the others. Pick out the best three and rewrite them until they are as crisp and funny as you can make them.

TROUBLESHOOTING

'I've tried to come up with a string of clever jokes from my ideagram, but they all seem a bit stupid and corny.'

You don't always have to be clever when writing jokes. Silly is great. Puns can be wonderful. It's a mistake to try and control your output too much. Let your subconscious take over a bit more. If your brain keeps suggesting stupid ideas, go with it. Write them down and you may find that some of them, with a bit more twisting and rewording, can become funny.

SUMMING UP

- Jokes have a simple setup–punchline structure.
- The punchline typically subverts the expectations of the setup.
- Jokes can be written using an ideagram for the base material.
- The topics on the ideagram can be turned into jokes using similar techniques to writing sketches.
- Wordplay is a great tool to use when writing jokes.
- The more jokes you attempt to write, the likelier you are to come up with a winner.

WRITING JOKES: BUILDING A ROUTINE

PERFORMING STANDUP COMEDY

Even if you don't think of yourself as a performer, give some thought to having a go at standup comedy. One of the best ways to test your jokes is to get up before a group of people and tell them yourself. There's no better way to advertise your writing talents – if you can make it work for you. In most major cities there's a club offering open-mic spots for beginners.

If you decide performance isn't for you, don't feel bad about yourself. Your skill is writing and that's what you're focusing on. But it's still worthwhile for you to read this chapter as it bears on writing joke-based comedy.

THE ART OF THE STANDUP COMEDIAN

As most comedians will tell you, their art is as much one of communication and empathy as it is of writing a string of brilliant gags. It's one that's learned the hard way, by taking your act before audiences and slowly learning to make them laugh.

- *Find your stage persona*: if you 'act' your routine as if you were presenting a character, the audience will sense the falsehood. Your performance should be idiosyncratically yours: your stage personality is a version of you, albeit exaggerated or subtly distorted.
- *Make your material personal*: you're expressing your vision, so talk about whatever makes you feel passionate. Even if you're telling a string of silly gags, it's the way you see things – it matters to you.
- *Doing a character act*: some comedians come on as a character who is distinct from their own personality – Al Murray the Pub

Landlord is an example of this. The character, though, should be someone whose skin you can slip into easily. They should sound as if they were talking spontaneously rather than reading a script.

THE FIVE-MINUTE ROUTINE

The new comedian's calling card for the club circuit is the five-minute act. It doesn't sound long, but it's plenty of time to let audiences know what you're all about. Don't underestimate the work you need to do to get your vehicle running and stage-worthy.

- *The opening*: the first ten seconds are vital. Your opening joke should introduce you, set the tone for your routine and make the audience laugh. If you have any peculiarities (we all have), this is the time to be open about them. It's the best way to get the punters on your side. For example, if you have a distinctive regional accent, write a joke about it, the area you come from or how you feel about your adopted part of the country.
- *The themes of the routine*: many routines riff through two or three topics, whether they are observational, surreal or confessional. You could be talking about a trip to the dentist and your relationship to your older sister: create your jokes by building an ideagram on each topic and segue from one to the other. Other comics tell disconnected jokes, others spin a long yarn. Find what suits you.
- *The rhythm of the routine*: a good routine will have regular and frequent laughs, ideally one about every ten seconds. A big laugh at the opening and the middle will build waves you can surf on. Plant a lot of lesser chuckles in between. These keep the comic energy going.
- *Ending the routine*: you'll want to go out on a high. Reserve one of your best jokes for the end. A good trick is to add an extra punchline to a joke you told earlier. If you want the compère to book you again, never go over your five minutes.

GETTING STARTED

There is much more to standup comedy than I've had space to describe here. There are courses across the country that could help you get started. Go to see as much standup as you can, in live shows rather than on TV. Acquaint yourself with what's happening out there, what works and what doesn't. Once you have your act up and running, don't let a bad gig discourage you. Everyone gets them. Be ready to learn, be brave and patient, and you never know where it may lead you.

If it's that split second too long, you will shave letters off of words. You will count syllables to get it just right. It's more like songwriting.

Jerry Seinfeld on writing jokes

WRITING SEVERAL JOKES ON THE SAME THEME

Ideagrams are very useful in building up a string of gags. Spread out visually, they help you cast your eye over the topics, making it easier for you to join things up, turn them around and generally play with them. It's a great way of creating linked jokes on a theme.

Imagine we're writing a routine about having had an unhappy childhood and needing therapy. This is always a great topic for humour: Woody Allen built half his career on it. Let's have a look at Figure 10. My eye lights on the NHS. We often think of psychoanalysis being exclusive and expensive. What if it was available on the NHS? Let's see what we can do with it.

GETTING SEVERAL PUNCHLINES OUT OF A SETUP

The current climate in the NHS is one of cuts. If we join up psychoanalysis and cuts what do we get?

'Digging up the source of your neuroses, a resource-strapped NHS psychoanalyst would only be able to take you back to the age of thirty-five.'

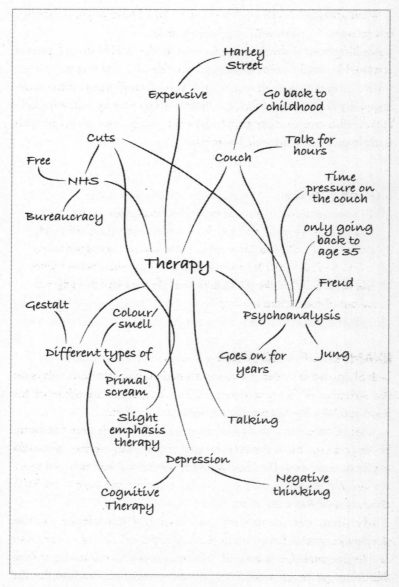

Figure 10

What about an NHS analyst's couch? You'd have to get off it after ten seconds to make way for someone else.

Looking round the ideagram, what if the NHS offered primal screams? It would become primal slight emphasis therapy.

It's not only labour-saving to spin several laughs out of the same setup. A good comic can create a wave of laughter by following one payoff with two or three more. This can delight the audience with a triple or even quadruple whammy.

> **→ NOW TRY THIS**
>
> To squeeze an extra joke out of a linked topic, look at the week's news. Is there anything there with which you can compare it? 'My dad's promise of extra pocket money was always overridden by my mum. A bit like how Nick Clegg and David Cameron behave with the country.' It'll make the routine fresh, but, as with this gag, will be out of date before too long.

EXAMPLE OF A ROUTINE

Jack Sheppard is a talented young comedian whose routine plays on the struggles of being a young male today. Here are some of his jokes followed by his notes on how he wrote them.

'A lot of people say that puberty was a really tough time for them. So fingers crossed, it'll never happen to me.' (*Sometimes the really simple options work best. Everyone tells me that I look very young for my age so I thought why not point out what the audience is probably thinking and make fun of myself.*')

'My first wet dream was a terrifying experience. I was sleepwalking and fell into the bath.' (*There are lots of phrases that can be interpreted in a number of ways . . . The setup makes it seem like it's going to be quite a crude joke so the punchline catches the audience out.*')

'I actually met my girlfriend at art college. We were drawn together.' *('I struggled for ages to come up with a good joke about meeting my girlfriend at art college. I watched a TV show called* Drawn Together *and the title seemed to work really well. I always try to keep my eye open as even the titles of books, films or TV shows can be made into something funny when given the right setup.')*

'I once went on a date and my parents happened to be there too. I was shocked. I didn't know they went to swingers' parties.' *('I think the top thing that would ruin a date would be seeing your parents there so I imagined the worst possible place for it to take place.')*

'My girlfriend's into bondage, but to be honest I'm not sure I want to get roped in to it. Sorry, that's not my best joke but I had to tie it in somehow.' *('I started by brainstorming all the various sexual practices I could think of. Bondage was one that struck me . . . because of the possible bits of wordplay. At first I wasn't too confident if the joke was very funny so I added in the second line and in the end both of them worked really well.')*

Writing is no trouble: you just jot down ideas as they occur to you. The jotting is simplicity itself – it's the occurring which is difficult.

Stephen Leacock, Canadian humorist

Exercise
Think of two topics and write ten jokes, five on each of them. Make the punchline for three of the jokes spring from the same setup.

TROUBLESHOOTING
'I'm writing a routine based on my personal experiences. Some of it is quite near the knuckle and I don't want to offend or hurt anyone'

Read the 'Giving Offence' section of Chapter 2 again. Comedy clubs are adult places and are very permissive about sexual material.

Your jokes about race, sexuality or religion are less likely to cause offence if they reflect a truth. However, being truthful in spirit doesn't mean that all the precise details of a routine have to come from real life. Audiences happily accept that the people in your routine are either fictional or fictionalized, so if you're talking about your partner they won't take everything as gospel truth. If your act does make fun of people you love, never mention them by name. You'd be wise not to invite them unless you're sure they'll take it in the right spirit.

SUMMING UP

- Many standup routines build jokes round a topic. Ideagrams are useful for this.
- A typical five-minute routine will segue between two or three topics.
- A good opening joke is vital.
- Try to get several punchlines out of one setup.
- At all times be true to yourself and what you're trying to say.

WRITING JOKES: FINDING OUTLETS FOR YOUR JOKES

PERFORMING STANDUP COMEDY

When you feel that your routine is ready, find your nearest comedy club, check whether they have a new-act night, and ring up and book a slot. You may well find this is months ahead. Use the time to rehearse, rewrite and polish your act.

WRITING FOR TOPICAL COMEDY SHOWS

The topical shows broadcast by the BBC which we looked at in Chapter 8 often include jokes about the news. Listen to the show carefully for the style, rhythm and subject matter, and the delivery of the performers. Pay particular attention to your phrasing: a word put in or taken out can make the difference between acceptance and rejection. Ask yourself:

- Do the jokes on the show follow a classic setup–punchline format?
- Are there a string of jokes on the same topic?
- What is the tone? Is it broad, clever, sarcastic, exuberant . . .?
- When are the deadlines?

Send in ten to twenty gags, all numbered and clearly spaced. Try to submit to every show in the series. A careful listen will help you understand the material and approach sought by the producers.

WRITING FOR PANEL SHOWS, QUIZZES AND GAME SHOWS

Many of these TV and radio programmes use jokes as part of the chairperson's chat. One-liners crop up regularly when the show is being introduced, a guest is brought on or as a link between different sections. They may not advertise themselves as open to non-commissioned submissions, but nevertheless eat up gags as fast as the weary writers can create them.

A quiz-show producer won't appreciate their inbox filled with unsuitable ideas which have obviously been sent scattershot, but may be willing to investigate a writer who can come up with a supply of well-crafted, funny gags that fit the show.

When you've built up a degree of confidence, consider sending some material on spec to a producer. Realistically, the high-profile TV shows probably won't look at your ideas. You stand a better chance with a comedy radio panel game or a show on a smaller TV channel. Of course, it's essential that your material fits the show in style, voice and subject matter. Write to the producer by name. If you can unearth some of their earlier work, give it a listen or a watch and tell them how much you enjoyed it.

WRITING FOR GREETINGS CARDS

TAPPING INTO A HUGE MARKET

Many cards use humour. After all, a greetings card comes in the perfect setup–punchline form: the outside sets up the gag and the inside delivers the payoff. The internet now plays a major part in the industry but the traditional card continues to flourish. If anything, the number of occasions they mark has grown: birthdays, weddings, engagements, leaving work, taking up a new job, moving abroad, a birth in the family, Valentine's Day, bereavement – the list goes on. What's more, the pay can be very worthwhile.

DO YOUR RESEARCH

It's no use sending a joke off to a company that only makes blank cards or submitting fart gags to one that specializes in verse. Browse in shops, look at what's on offer online and find who uses the kind of humour you could write. Find out more about the industry by going to trade fairs and reading the trade magazines.

Closely study the style and wording used by every company. You may think cards are easy to write but it takes practice and skill to give the publisher exactly what they are looking for.

SUBMITTING YOUR COPY

Card companies plan their publications months ahead. If you have ideas for Christmas, you will probably need to submit your copy in July. Good timing is essential.

Ring or write to the publisher asking for their writers' guidelines. Make sure you enclose a stamped addressed envelope and follow their directions to the letter. Just as with other forms of comedy writing, it may take you several tries before you find success.

WRITING FOR THE INTERNET

If you type in 'jokes' on Google you get over 30,000,000 results. There are millions of websites publishing gags of all types and in all languages. Some of them welcome submissions from writers, very few of them pay. You won't make yourself a comedy career by providing fodder for internet sites, but some sites are worth your while.

Cracked.com is a US topical humour site that pays writers well and has a huge number of visitors. The style of humour and many of the references are American, so study the style and content thoroughly. Most of the published pieces are in the spoof news-article genre rather than one-liners, but the skills you have developed writing topical sketches will come in good stead here.

NewsBiscuit was founded by Spitting Image writer John O'Farrell. Every article and joke on this topical satire site is written by readers and, although there is no pay, the site gives full credits and is good exposure.

DeadBrain is another UK topical satire site which uses a lot of writers. Again, there is no pay but writers are credited and the standard of humour is high.

WRITING FOR THE PRESS

Some magazines and newspapers actively solicit one-liners from the wider public. They may not give you 'cool' credibility, if that's what you want, but many will pay, sometimes handsomely. They are frequently women's magazines in the middle range of the market. They accept ideas from men, but to be successful you must get inside the minds of the readership. A women's weekly with a warm, feelgood style is not going to publish a knob gag, even if it's brilliant. Study three copies of the magazine to get a feel for what it publishes before submitting your jokes.

Reader's Digest is worth a specific mention because it pays so well. Every month it features funny stories, some 'from life', others as straightforward gags. They also solicit jokes on their website. As with everything else in comedy – I hope this is beginning to sink in – you need to study the market for style, content and approach.

WRITING FOR COMEDIANS

These days comedians like to write their own material. Standup comedy has become more confessional and comedians want complete control of their act. I hate to put a damper on your ambition, but sending a hopeful round-robin batch of gags to every famous comedian you know of will probably get you nowhere.

However, if you come across a talented new comic who shares your comedy vision, it could be worth your while collaborating. Remember that it's they who put themselves in the line of fire, so it's reasonable for them to have the final say on their material. You won't get rich doing this, but you'll quickly gain a priceless education in comedy.

WEB TIPS

For more tips on writing jokes, go to www.tonykirwood.co.uk/index.php/script-writing

SUMMING UP

- The main outlets for jokes and one-liners are BBC topical shows, game and quiz shows, greetings cards, the internet, and print magazines and newspapers.
- Finding a comedian to write for is difficult, and it works best when you have a mutual understanding and empathy.

WRITING SITCOMS: THE DIFFERENT TYPES OF SITCOM

WHY WRITE A SITCOM?

CAPTURING THE ZEITGEIST

Sitcoms are the Golden Fleece for comedy writers. A successful series can turn you from an unknown into someone who's in constant demand and whose work is given the attention and respect it is due. A series that just does okay will still be a formidable addition to your CV.

Sitcom characters exert a powerful grip on our imagination. They enter millions of living rooms week after week to entertain us and reflect our lives back to us. We get to know them like our own family, their failings are our failings, they can be beautifully performed by terrific actors and, of course, they're funny.

'Show . . . the very age and body of the time his form and pressure.' That's what actors do, according to Shakespeare. He could have been talking about sitcoms. The 1960s generation gap with *Steptoe and Son*, the 1990s New Lads with *Men Behaving Badly*, the stresses of 2000s parenthood with *Outnumbered* – if you want to capture the times and make people laugh, write a sitcom.

CREATING CHARACTERS

Characters are at the heart of a sitcom. Whether they are sweethearts or monsters (usually a bit of both), they permeate the audience's imagination and concentrate the writer's efforts. Nothing allows you to luxuriate in character as much as a sitcom – providing you place them in the right situation and get them to interact in funny and truthful ways.

FINDING AN IDEA

Building a sitcom concept is different from getting sketch or joke ideas. You can't do it by suddenly crystallizing an idea and jotting it down. The process is slower and more organic: bit by bit you build the framework, adding and subtracting, until you think it's strong enough to carry the whole edifice. On the way, you'll add and remove elements and rethink aspects of your piece. It's something you can't rush.

STARTING WITH A CHARACTER

Perhaps you have a person or a group of people knocking inside your brain trying to get out. Keep thinking about them and start to get to know them better. The next chapter will help you do this.

STARTING WITH A LOCATION

Maybe your starting point is a place, very possibly a work environment: a veterinary surgery, for example, a hospital ward or a boiler service control room. Perhaps you've worked in one and see the comic possibilities. That's fine. Your next step is to think about the characters who people it and how they interact in that location.

STARTING WITH A SITUATION

Or perhaps you've hit upon a situation that has a contemporary ring, for example a recession-hit family in which three generations are forced to live under one roof. Again, that's fine, but go back to the characters.

STARTING WITH A STYLE

You have a vision of a guerrilla-style series filmed with a hand-held camera about a group of graffiti writers. Great! But you know what I'm going to say . . . go back to the characters.

SITUATIONS TO AVOID

It's far easier to talk about the setups you should avoid than it is to outline what will work. No one knows what could become the next

Miranda or *The Office*. If we did, everyone would be doing it. But let's get the negatives out of the way.

- *Ideas that have flopped*: settings of sitcoms that have done a nosedive will be no-go areas for several years. This was the case with historical themes, which have only just become permissible again. Check your idea isn't too close to one that has failed in the last few years.
- *Very successful ideas*: conversely, if your idea is close to that of a recent big hit, you're in danger of looking unoriginal or at least of swimming in its wake. After *Peep Show*, it's inadvisable for a while to write a sitcom about two dysfunctional flat-sharing males – unless it's very original.
- *'High concept' ideas*: these are ones that are complicated, overwrought and possibly time-limited. For example, your family live in a house under which a band of robbers are digging a tunnel to get at the bank next door. There are obvious comic possibilities, but they don't add up to a sitcom. It will get resolved too quickly and the situation overrides the characters. Besides which, you will have too many characters who never interact.

Everything human is pathetic. The secret source of humour itself is not joy but sorrow.

Mark Twain

PLANNING YOUR SITCOM

Nobody can dream up a hit sitcom and dash it off in a fortnight. You're probably going to spend weeks labouring over your concept, choosing your characters, building their conflicts and planning episodes before writing a line of dialogue. You need to be passionate about your subject matter, as you'll be living with it for months.

The more carefully you lay your foundations, the stronger the structure you build on it. Your efforts in the early stages are well worthwhile. If you dash off the dialogue straight away without meticulously planning where you are going, you could find in a few weeks that you've written yourself into a blind alley from which you can see no way out. After immersing yourself in your characters and their conflicts and honing and re-honing your concept, your dialogue and scenes will flow much easier.

BEING REALISTIC

At this point it's very important to be clear what is likely to happen to your finished sitcom when, after weeks or months of painstaking work, you send it off to a broadcaster. If you have shown talent, passion and a real feel for comedy, you may well be called in for a meeting with one of the producers and begin a fruitful relationship that could lead to you becoming part of a team on an existing sitcom or, even better, to a full production of your own sitcom.

It's unlikely, though, that this, your first sitcom, will be the one that is broadcast. Don't exhale loudly and say, 'What's the point of writing something that isn't going to see the light of day?' The work you will be doing on it will be immensely important. See it as your calling card for the industry: your showcase episode. You will show the people who matter that you have the talent, the vision and the staying power to write a sitcom. It's your first vital step. Put every ounce of your passion and comic insight into your writing, and who knows where it will lead you?

ESTABLISHING THE STYLE

Decide early on what type of sitcom you want to write. This will affect the texture, the type of humour and the quality of your characterization. Let's have a look at the choices.

DOING AWAY WITH THE LAUGH TRACK

- *Filming without a studio audience*: nowadays watchers and listeners are less willing to chuckle at recorded laughter. They don't want to feel that the actors are playing up to the crowd. They need their behaviour to be more natural and true to life. The most important aspects of this kind of sitcom are:

o The humour is less broad. Situations can be more realistic.

o There are no obvious setups and gags.

o Scenes can be shorter.

o The visual language, the editing and pacing, is more like film.

o There is no hiatus between the scenes shot in the studio and the pre-recorded filmed sequences of earlier sitcoms.

• *Filming can be liberating*: filmed comedy doesn't have to be grainily realistic. For example, in *Peep Show* the two main characters Jeremy and Mark deliver non-naturalistic monologues to the camera, which wouldn't have been possible in a studio setup. In *Flight of the Conchords* Bret and Jermaine break into stylized, filmed song and dance numbers. This style allows you to be highly creative.

USING A LAUGH TRACK

Some sitcoms such as *Miranda* and *Mrs Brown's Boys* have gone back into the studio with huge success. Sitcoms filmed before an audience have:

• Broad gags, often visual, at frequent intervals. The traditional setup–punchline rhythm is used much more.

• Broader characters. They need to be instantly and constantly funny to keep the audience laughing.

• Limited locations. A typical studio-based sitcom will be filmed on a set with no more than five or six settings, which could be sitting rooms, bedrooms, pubs, cafés or offices.

WRITING FOR RADIO

Think hard about whether your idea could work for radio. You may see it as less glamorous, but as a new writer you stand a much better chance of being broadcast here than on TV. It's a highly creative, if challenging, medium. Radio sitcoms have as much variety and follow much the same 'rules' as their TV counterparts. Radio, though, as we saw in Chapter 5, has its own specific challenges and advantages.

Talking to a BBC commissioner we were told that every time a new style of comedy comes out she would be inundated with scripts which were little more than ersatz versions. Originality is essential. They should always try and find their authentic voice.

Paul Minett and Brian Leveson, writers of *Booze Cruise*,
My Family and *Oh Doctor Beeching!*

ESTABLISHING YOUR FORMAT

SINGLE MAIN CHARACTER

Many sitcoms are about the trials and foibles of one central character. David Brent in *The Office* springs to mind, as well as *Frasier* or *Miranda*.

- The character is larger than life and we get to know them in detail.
- They are the motor of all the main storylines and most of the comedy.
- They can be sympathetic or a monster but must be compelling and funny enough to hold the audience's attention for at least six episodes.
- Other characters will be important inasmuch as they interact with them.

SMALL GROUP OF CHARACTERS

Here the dynamic is fuelled by the conflicts between a small number of people – usually two, three or four. Classic examples are *Steptoe and Son*, more recently *Peep Show* or *Friday Night Dinner*.

- The comedy springs from their interaction. All storylines will be about their recurring and unsolvable conflicts.
- Individual characters may dominate less than in the single main character format, but they are defined by their relationships with each other.
- They are locked in a close situation with each other, such as family, flat-sharers or co-workers.
- There will be a constant bone of contention between them, whether it is closely or loosely defined.
- Other regular characters exist to bring out the foibles of the main group.

LARGER GROUP OF CHARACTERS

We follow the misadventures of a band of people who are all more or less equally featured. *Cheers* is a classic group sitcom. *Benidorm* is a more recent example.

- The characters are bound together in a situation, typically at work, or in an organization or a restricted environment such as a small village.
- Individual episodes may be about one or two of them but throughout the series they all have equal billing.
- Although their ties may be slightly less tight than in the small group sitcom, they will all nevertheless have a compelling reason to remain together.
- The characters will be of a wide variety of types to add colour to the comedy and variety to the storylines.
- As in all sitcoms, the comedy is fuelled by the characters' ceaseless conflict.

Exercise

Think of six sitcoms you know that have been made in the last fifteen years. For each one, ask yourself, what type of sitcom is it? What situation glues the characters together? If you have an idea for a sitcom in the back of your mind, ask yourself what overall type it is likely to fall into. Recorded with or without an audience? Single character, small or larger group? Don't make any hard or fast decisions just yet. Envisage a few scenes from an episode. What feels best?

TROUBLESHOOTING

'I've an idea for a sitcom based in a very wacky location. I'm sure the brilliant setting will make it work. Do I really have to do all this initial work on how many characters I need?'

Stand back from your idea for a minute. Apart from your wonderful setting, do you have any idea of what your storylines might entail or how the characters will interact? Will the setting by itself keep the audience entertained over six episodes?

Examine the people who inhabit your location. Which ones could be the mainspring of the action and how many of them are there? How could you build a sitcom round them? Does the crazy setting enhance them or get in their way? If it's the latter, choose a more mundane one.

SUMMING UP

- Character is at the heart of sitcom.
- Find a theme and characters about which you are passionate.
- Sitcoms take a good deal of planning.
- Establish early whether it will be a studio-recorded or filmed sitcom.
- Decide whether it will be a single main character or group sitcom.

13
WRITING SITCOMS: CREATING YOUR CHARACTERS

SITCOM CHARACTER ESSENTIALS

From the formation of your idea to the moment you type 'Ends' at the bottom of the script, keep your characters in the centre of your vision, watching them, shaping them and sometimes losing them or creating new ones.

CHARACTERS IN DIFFERENT GENRES

In sketches, films and sitcoms, characters follow a different process. See Figure 11.

- *Movie characters*: the hero goes through an arc of change. By the end of the story, their struggle will have transformed them, whether it's a comedy like *Groundhog Day* or an action movie like *Terminator*.
- *Sketch characters*: these people, on the other hand, don't change at all. Their response to every situation is invariable. They are funny because we know exactly what they are going to do.
- *Sitcom characters*: they may undergo some changes throughout an episode and may even display an unexpected reaction or two, but in the end they revert to their psychological status quo.

SUCCESSFUL SITCOM CHARACTERS

It follows that leading characters in a sitcom need to be:

- *Compelling*: unless there is something uniquely fascinating, awesome, lovable or repellent about them, the audience will lose interest. They must make us want to return to them time after time.

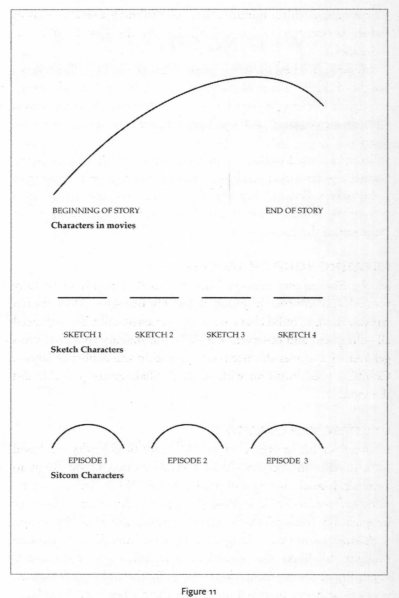

BEGINNING OF STORY   END OF STORY
Characters in movies

SKETCH 1   SKETCH 2   SKETCH 3   SKETCH 4
Sketch Characters

EPISODE 1   EPISODE 2   EPISODE 3
Sitcom Characters

Figure 11

- *Layered*: over thirty minutes, they need to show several aspects to their personality, which are brought to the fore in different situations.
- *Repetitive*: if they undergo drastic changes, the audience loses sight of them. Sitcom characters exist in a kind of mobile stasis.
- *Original*: cliché is the death of comedy. Just one character who is purely stereotypical or lifted from other sitcoms could mar your series.
- *Funny*: a central character must, of course, be very funny. Many other regular characters, however, are not particularly amusing in themselves. Perhaps they provide a sympathetic presence or are a bouncing board for the others. This is why being funny is not at the top of the list.

CREATING YOUR CHARACTER

Maybe Shakespeare allowed Falstaff to drift into his mind fully formed and effortlessly jotted down his dialogue. Most mortal writers, though, build characters more systematically. You will need all your talent and observational skills, but making your characters gel over six episodes also needs craftsmanship and deliberate labour. Combine your intuition with method. Shakespeare probably did the same.

CONCEIVING YOUR CHARACTER

Drawn from life or dreamt up in your head? Basil Fawlty was based on a hotelier in Torquay. Ricky Gervais created David Brent to entertain himself during dull patches in his DJ job. There is no 'by numbers' method of corralling the people who march into your imagination. It doesn't matter whether your inspiration comes from a chance encounter, a longstanding acquaintance or a random thought. It's likely that it will be a combination. If no one is appearing at the moment, don't worry. By the end of this chapter, you will be better prepared to nurture them when they do arrive.

BUILDING THE CHARACTER

You may well begin with a vague image and possibly a phrase or two. A good way to bring this person into focus is to ask questions about them. The questionnaire below will help you. You needn't answer the questions in their strict order, but answer all of them as fully as you can. Sometimes a character will grow unaided in your unconscious mind, sometimes they need some coaxing: either way, this will help firm them up. At this stage it's all work in progress: you're not coming to hard-and-fast decisions just yet. It's like doing a sketch for a painting that can be altered or erased at any time.

- *What is their main attitude?* In other words, how do they relate to the world and the people around them? Are they embittered, hopeful or confused? David Brent in *The Office* wants to ingratiate himself with his staff as a jokey, relaxed man of the people whose staff love him. It colours everything he does and says.
- *What is their secondary attitude?* People have layers. We operate on different levels that are sometimes contradictory. Someone might be overbearing in the office but have an underlying insecurity that makes them submissive with their partner. David Brent wants to be approachable but also has an insensitivity that blinds him to people's reactions.
- *Name three character traits:* identify how they behave. Some of these traits will be apparent to all, others only to a few people who are close to them. They will be a defining part of the character. So three of David Brent's traits are a forced jokiness, a deluded sense of his talent and an insensitivity to people's feelings.
- *Name three noticeable habits*: these can add details that make your character memorable. They can be immediately obvious, such as a pompous way of talking to people you want to impress, or miniscule, like blowing up at your hair while trying to think. These habits may propel a scene or even an episode, or not be

revealed in the script at all. They will all make the character more vivid in your imagination.

- *What do they want out of life?* This will affect their behaviour in every episode. Their desires motivate them and are the source of their hopes and despair. They bring them into conflict with the other characters. Sometimes this overarching need is something specific: David Brent wants to use the docusoap to make himself a star. Often it is more general: for example, the character wants to find love.
- *What stops them getting it?* We're now getting to the heart of things. No successful sitcom has yet been made about someone who is completely satisfied with their life and who has achieved all their goals. Dissatisfaction and thwarted desire drive the inhabitants of British sitcomland – and, in their own way, their American cousins. The obstacle may be another character but it could just as well be the psyche of the person themselves. David Brent won't achieve his dreams because he doesn't have the talent.
- *How do they interact with the other characters?* At this stage you may only have the vaguest idea of who else will populate your sitcom. It's still worth asking how your character behaves with them, however ghostly they may be, and what she or he thinks about them. They will be the people with whom they share their life. Answering this may give you ideas for stories.
- *Their passport details*:
  - Their name;
  - Their gender;
  - Their job;
  - Their marital status;
  - Their sexual orientation which, fortunately, is not information demanded for our passports, but may be central to a character's outlook on life.

Spend some time on your character's name. Think how perfectly Victor Meldrew, Edina Monsoon and Alan Partridge fit the character. Don't rush: it may help to give them a try-out name while you're thinking.

- *What do they like about themselves?* This can be the very thing that others dislike about them, so asking this can sound out their level of self-delusion.
- *What do they dislike about themselves?* This gives us an insight into their vulnerability, a very important factor in building a sitcom character. It may well be something they never reveal to others.
- *What is their secret?* We all have them. Sometimes they're trivial, sometimes they're horrendous. Often they're very surprising. Knowing this will help you build a richer and funnier character. Again, it may be something no one else knows.
- *What is their history so far?* Write 200–300 words on their life story. You may never use this in a script, so don't over-elaborate. But you may discover something crucial.

It's straightforward stuff: character, character, character. You don't need jokes, you don't need funny lines. The humour will come because the secret to the truly funny sitcoms is simple – they are basically all about life.

Barry Cryer, writing in the Radio Times

Exercise

Ask all these questions about a well-known sitcom character.

> **→ NOW TRY THIS**
> Imagine being introduced to your character at a party. Are they shy or confident? Do they try to find out about you or do they talk about themselves? What are they drinking and how much have they had?

THE COMIC FLAW

Sitcom characters are rarely well-balanced, satisfied, likable and successful all at the same time. Such people may be good to know in life but are uninteresting and unfunny on TV and radio. However lovable your main characters, there will be something in their nature that undermines their path through life. The flaw could be unattractive, such as Basil Fawlty's snobbery. It is often likable, such as Pete and Sue Brockman's excessive desire to be fair to their children in *Outnumbered*. Whatever it is, their flaw is one of the reasons why we keep tuning in to watch a character. It is also why they keep striving week after week.

Exercise

Now start to build a character. Treat them the same whether they're part of a sitcom you want to write, or someone you want to develop just for the sake of the exercise. Shut your eyes for five minutes and imagine them acting and talking. Do this a second time if they are still somewhat vague. Then answer the first seven questions of the questionnaire about them.

CREATING CONFLICT

There's no story without conflict. This is true of novels, fairytales and plays. It's what makes human interaction compelling. Characters need to be tested and put under stress or else we quickly lose interest. Their struggles shape the development and resolution of the story. Our sympathy for them depends largely on the way they cope with the pressure.

MAKE THE CONFLICT SPRING FROM THE CHARACTER

The engine for sitcom plots is the never-ending struggle between the characters, albeit given new twists each week. The characters don't need to be aggressive people: a placid person pushed unwillingly into permanent struggle can be a great source of comedy.

Some types of conflict are:

- Two people want the same thing.
- A person wants something but another person wants to prevent them getting it.
- Someone is presented with an obstacle and someone else prevents them overcoming it.
- Someone has internal conflicts that prevent them attaining their goal.
- Someone tries to help another person with a problem or to achieve a goal but only makes it worse.
- Someone wants someone else to behave in a particular way but they won't.

Desire and problem-solving are at the heart of conflict. The desire can be for something concrete, such as wanting someone sexually who won't reciprocate, or it can be for an emotional state, such as wanting an enjoyable evening but someone else is behaving embarrassingly.

Conflict can be understated or even unexpressed. In *The Office*, Tim and Dawn find David Brent very annoying, but they rarely come into confrontation with him.

> **→ NOW TRY THIS**
> Imagine your character trapped in a lift. Do they panic? Are they calm? Do they use humour? Again, close your eyes and imagine them. Now imagine the other characters. How do they react to the first character? Do they say anything? Are they polite, calm or angry with them? How does this develop?

Exercise

Ask the remaining questions about your character.

SITCOM TRY-OUT

Let's see how this works with an idea I have for a sitcom character.

THE MAIN CHARACTER

She's touching forty and painfully aware of it. I see her as having artistic aspirations but frustrated in a humdrum office job. Her attitude to life is caustic and her views are strong. She is desperate to make contacts in the arts but her sharp tongue gets in the way of her success. She sees cant everywhere: unfortunately, she's trying to make headway in a world where there is a lot of it. Her affectionate relationships with her few friends quickly turn to sarcasm at their shortcomings. She tuts and drums her fingers quite a lot. She's quite vivid in my mind, and I see her as being the central part of the sitcom. I'll call her Cass. Cassandra is a loner and has a negative view of things.

I want Cass to work somewhere where she's constantly reminded of her artistic ambitions and frustrations. In a film production company? The leisure services department of a council? I'll settle on an arts centre. I'll make her the courses manager. It's the kind of thing she'd do. However, the job in itself won't satisfy her.

THE OTHER MAIN CHARACTERS

- *The arts centre director*: I'll call him Gavin. I see him as a trendy, youngish type who spouts a lot of arts management jargon – perhaps he's done a university course in it. This would really irritate Cass. Gavin hates conflict and is passively emollient (he calls it 'positive'). He's ambitious and sees himself running a major arts festival, but isn't very competent and easily loses control of difficult people. He thinks he's managing everyone very well by repeating mantras such as 'I'm really excited about this.'
- *The arts centre buildings manager*: he's a tradesman who's landed what he thinks is a cushy job. Desi, as I'll call him, is his late forties, cynical, with a cheerful demeanour with which he tries to disarm

people. It's a weapon he needs because he's very lazy. He used to go round changing light bulbs to make himself look busy, but now he has his own office he only has to shuffle a few papers. He's competent but will put off tackling jobs until it's nearly too late.

- *Cass's flatmate*: I feel Cass needs a sounding board. A domestic life will give her a more rounded character. Clive is a long-term friend since university, but hasn't got very far in life. He lives in his head and lacks drive. He is obsessed with humidity and regularly retreats to his room to take readings.

CREATING SECONDARY CHARACTERS

Secondary characters may feature in every episode or only occasionally. Although they are rarely centre stage, they can have a major impact on the success of a series.

Secondary characters are invaluable because:

- *They add realism*: whether they are neighbours, occasional friends or colleagues, they ground the situation in the real world.
- *They add colour*: sprinkle a few different types among your supporting cast to enrich the texture and add more opportunities for comedy.
- *They add opportunities for storylines*: the actions of a minor character can snowball into a situation that involves the main personnel. They are invaluable in keeping plots moving.
- *You can bounce your main characters off them*: a well-placed secondary character gives you opportunities to reveal more facets of your main ones.

TYPES OF SECONDARY CHARACTER

- *The crazies*: many sitcoms are enriched by characters who are so weird as to be barely human. They may be neighbours, workmates or friends: a peripheral presence but enough to impinge on the main characters' lives. Major Gowan in *Fawlty*

Towers, Warren in *Porridge* and Jim and his dog Wilson in *Friday Night Dinner* are all at the extreme end of the spectrum but contribute hugely to the comedy. Here are some attributes of crazy characters:

o Their one extreme characteristic is all we see of them. In this respect, they are much like sketch characters.
o They live on the edge of the main characters' lives.
o The audience has little empathy for them but they can add a vital foil for the other characters.
o They can be relied on to raise a laugh and are an invaluable tool to add comedy when it is needed.
o They can help drive the plot, particularly if you want something to go wrong. Crazies add to the mayhem or can be the fly in the ointment.
o Crazy characters can make a sitcom wearing and less believable if overused.

If you feel your sitcom is over-full of rounded, sympathetic people, ask yourself if a crazy could add some comic zest.

• *Friends and allies*: confidants and confidantes help the audience understand and empathize with the emotions of the main character. They often aren't very funny in their own right but can make a series more watchable.

o They're a sounding board to the main character, someone who gives them a chance to express their needs.
o They need to be characterized in their own right. If they are simply functional, the audience will turn off.

• *Monsters*: like crazies, monsters are painted with a broad brush. But while crazies can be lovable, monsters are distinctly unsympathetic. They add tension to the storylines, increase the stress of the characters and can be funny in their own right. Needless to say, they are normally antagonistic to the main character. Terrifying or just appalling, they're the people we love to hate. Great sitcom monsters are David Brent's obnoxious salesman friend Finchy in *The Office*, Grouty, the gangster who controls the prison in *Porridge*, and Angela, Sue's vindictive, manipulative sister in *Outnumbered*. Some characteristics of monsters:

o They are wholly unsympathetic.

o They add to the problems of the main cast and raise the stakes.

o They show the main character in a more sympathetic light. They will always be the most unpleasant and possibly frightening person on the scene.

o They are a powerful but not necessarily ubiquitous presence in the lives of the main characters.

o They can help to kick off and develop storylines.

These characters can give a sitcom more drive and add drama to an episode.

> **→ NOW TRY THIS**
>
> Even if you're not an artist, do some drawings of your secondary characters. They may well come out as caricatures – that's fine. What impression do they make? Do they have any outstanding or unusual facial or bodily characteristics? Although the character as performed probably won't look much like your sketch, doing this will help you form a clearer picture of them.

The other big mistake comes when writers fail to ask the key questions! Does this scene advance the plot or advance the character development? If not, it's doing nothing! Sure it might be funny but it should also work. A final useful tip is to 'cast' any script in your head. Pick actors who would be perfect for the part. It doesn't matter if you can't afford them, because the purpose of this exercise is to stop all the characters sounding like you! When you write, you should be able to hear their voice and their inflections.

Paul Minett and Brian Leveson

Exercise

Now imagine the people with whom your character interacts. Let a few possibilities drift through your mind. Pick out one or two who seem the most promising. Allow yourself time to visualize them and get to know them a little. Now ask yourself how they interact with the first character.

USING STATUS

In almost every situation in life someone has the upper hand, even amongst ostensible equals. It can vary in different situations or even at different times of the day. An understanding of how it plays in your characters' lives will add a rich layer to the comedy.

STATUS AT WORK

If yours is a work-located sitcom, what are your characters' places in the hierarchy? What do they think about this? Do they try to do anything to change or to preserve it?

STATUS IN EVERYDAY LIFE

We regularly interact with doctors, bank managers, shop assistants, policemen and bartenders. How does your character deal with these people? Do they feel above or below them? Are any of them regular characters?

STATUS WITHIN THE FAMILY

We are expected to look up to parents and, to a lesser extent, older siblings. We defer to grandparents in a different kind of way. How do your characters negotiate these strands of status? Does any of this inspire ideas for stories?

STATUS BETWEEN PEERS

People are never completely equal. There is rarely absolute parity in a marriage or friendship. One partner holds the purse strings, another the TV remote. One friend will be the more successful. One flat-sharer will pay the rent or organize the rotas. The difference may be psychological. Sybil Fawlty holds the whip hand over Basil because she has a better business sense and doesn't share his unrealistic aspirations.

REVERSED STATUS

Power relationships are ripe for overturning. Jim Hacker in *Yes Minister* fights a losing battle with civil servant Sir Humphrey, nominally his underling. In *Outnumbered* parents Pete and Sue are under the thumb of their three children. A manager who is over-anxious to please his staff or a patient who cows her psychiatrist with insights into his inner nature, for example, could make great comedy.

Examine your characters' status, whatever their relationship. You will discover things about them and will have a richer idea of how they interact.

SITCOM TRY-OUT

I need another character or two to bring the arts centre alive:

- *The receptionist*: to add colour I see her as American. She's nineteen, naive and optimistic, from the Midwest. She's not very bright, but has a heart of gold and is a great conflict solver. She annoys the sceptical Brits at the arts centre with her homespun Midwestern philosophy, but is so sweet that their resistance melts. She will do anything to help, but unfortunately is out of her depth in the job and is constantly messing up. But her smiles almost make up for it. She definitely believes in angels. Candy is a name which seems to suit her.

Make sure you watch lots of comedy! And do this with other people. Sounds simple but what you find funny may not have universal appeal so it's a good discipline to start observing and digesting comic trends.

Lynne Parker, founder of Funny Women,
a UK organization devoted to promoting female comedy

Exercise

Answer the questionnaire in 'Building the character' on each of the secondary characters you have chosen.

TROUBLESHOOTING

'I'm in the early stage of conceiving a character. Doing the questionnaire seems like awfully hard work and actually seems to get in the way of me imagining them.'

Do the questionnaire in tandem with your creative visualization and don't approach it as if it were a series of boxes that have to be ticked. If your character is appearing in your mind very strongly, focus on that first and then ask the questions to consolidate them. However, if a character seems to be springing up more reluctantly, doing the questionnaire early on should help you build them. Use your instincts throughout and take your time.

SUMMING UP

- Although layered, sitcom characters don't change.
- Sitcom characters need a distinctive predominant attitude.
- They need to be in conflict with the other regular characters.
- They need to want something out of life that powers the storylines.
- Decide what secondary characters you need and what types they are.
- Use status to help determine the interplay between the characters.

14
WRITING SITCOMS: NAILING YOUR PREMISE

WHAT'S YOUR THEME?

Every drama, from a sketch to a Shakespearian tragedy, has a theme. This is a kind of invisible subtitle of which the audience may barely be conscious but which nevertheless colours their response.

A theme is, by nature, abstract but can be described in a few words. I'd say *Brokeback Mountain* is about forbidden love; *Fawlty Towers* about thwarted aspiration; *The Office* about self-delusion. You may word these differently and add secondary themes: for example, *The Office* is also a satire on modern management styles. But after some thought, you should be able to describe the theme of any sitcom, film or novel in a phrase or two.

Now's the time to ask yourself about your overall theme. It may seem quite abstract, and not the stuff of comedy, but having a picture of your big idea will clarify and add weight to your concept.

I always struggle to come up with a convincing answer when people ask me 'Where do you get your ideas from?' The fact is that the ideas are normally rather banal; it's what you do with them that counts.

Simon Nye, describing the writing of
his hit sitcom *Men Behaving Badly*

ESTABLISHING THE TRAP

Your characters do not simply share a space. They need to be joined by a permanent chain that they can't break. This chain keeps them fighting, making love, yearning and bickering with each other episode after episode. If any of your main characters can simply walk out and leave, the audience will subliminally lose interest. The trap that grips your characters is at the heart of your sitcom.

Perhaps the most perfect trap in sitcom history is Slade Green prison in *Porridge*, a place from which there is, in a literal sense, no escape. Most traps, though, are economic and/or emotional, but no less strong for not being physical.

THE FAMILY

None of us can escape our family. Even when we've grown up, relationships with our siblings, parents and our own children pervade our lives. I can't think of a stronger single influence on the way we are. And this is before we get to talk about aunts, uncles, cousins . . .

- *The difficult marriage*: this is the motor of many sitcoms. If your characters are trapped in one, ask yourself why they don't simply break up. Maybe they still, deep down, love each other. Perhaps there are economic or social reasons. Basil Fawlty, for example, knows he couldn't run the hotel without Sybil. Don't underestimate the force of habit, especially with older people. Margaret Meldrew in *One Foot in the Grave* has learnt over the years to put up with Victor's ranting. There are hints of a lost child and the shared grief that binds them together. They are also old, a time when separation is emotionally and financially more damaging. In a sense, their trap is old age.
- *Parents and children*: writers are often urged to 'write what you know'. We've all been children, many of us have them, and have felt the victimhood of unfairness, the generation gap or the burden of responsibility. These sometimes rocky, sometimes loving, relationships are made the more fruitful for sitcoms by being so hard to walk away from. There are many aspects to the parent/child relationship. Here are a few:

- o Embarrassment;
- o Dependency;
- o Control;
- o Rebellion (coming from either party);
- o Family rituals;
- o Social expectation;
- o Obligations.
- *Siblings*: the mixture of affection and rivalry in sibling relationships is rich for comedy. After all, a sister or brother isn't just for Christmas. These relations can give a sitcom its heart, as with Del and Rodney Trotter in *Only Fools and Horses*, or a bit of spike with Sue and Angela in *Outnumbered*.

Many sitcoms are about people with no blood links whatever. But even these can be given shape by introducing a family element: for example, in *Porridge*, Godber fell in love with Fletcher's daughter when she was visiting.

WORK

In the second great sitcom trap, the ties would seem to be economic. We feel we will never get out of our office, factory or daily round because we have to pay the mortgage. We often stay put, though, for more than merely financial reasons.

- *Find the emotional trap*: anyone can leave a job at any time; we endure wage labour rather than slavery. We get stuck in a work environment to fulfil all kinds of need. Inertia, fear, misplaced ambition or a simple lack of imagination all keep people turning up to the same office each day at 9.30.
- *Make the trap spring from the character*: in *The Office* Tim is trapped because, although bright, he's scared of taking a risk, while Gareth stays because he looks up to David. There are environments that are intrinsically harder to leave such as the Army, a prison or a weather station. Make sure these traps are echoed deep inside the characters.

FLAT SHARE

There have been flat-sharing sitcoms since the dawn of the form. Tony Hancock fantasizes while Sid James sniggers in their shared house in Railway Cuttings. Mark and Jeremy squabble over the kitchen table in *Peep Show*. Fifty years divide these two classics but in essence they are about lonely men who need each other's company.

The flat-share setting offers a source of endless conflict as a group of ill-matched people live in each other's sitting-, bath- and sometimes bedrooms. It can incorporate divergences of lifestyle, background, region and culture which are not seen in most families.

What holds these people together? It could be student poverty (*The Young Ones*) or, in *Men Behaving Badly*, the laddish need of Gary and Tony to huddle and get drunk together as protection from their women.

Exercise

Think of three sitcoms you know well. What is their overall theme? What is the trap that holds the characters together? Is it a physical, economic or emotional one? Do the characters have different traps? Now look at the sitcom you are building. Ask yourself what the theme is. Now try to describe the trap. Does it apply to all the characters? If not, how are the others bound into the situation? Is the trap lasting and solid, and is it reflected in the characters? Keep reminding yourself that it's all work-in-progress.

→ NOW TRY THIS

Think of your characters as belonging to a family even if they're not related. Who are the 'parents' with authority? How do the other characters (the 'children') react? Do they act like brothers and sisters? Who is bossy/supportive/jealous? Many groups have a whipping order much like that of a family. Are there any avuncular or grandparent figures?

ESTABLISHING THE SETTING

Think hard about the locations of your sitcom. Viewers will be watching or listeners will be imagining them week after week. More than a mere backdrop for the characters, they are as important a part of their emotional environment as their relationships.

USING A LIMITED NUMBER OF SETS

In the not so distant past, every sitcom was recorded in a studio split into five or six sets: typically the sitting room, the kitchen, the hall, the main characters' bedroom and the pub down the road. Nearly every scene was shot on one of these sets before an audience. Extra 'external' scenes were filmed on location and spliced into the final edit. The joins sometimes showed.

Nowadays, film values predominate and the style is more fluid. There is greater ease of moving from one room to another and going outside. But the principle remains: limit the number of sets. It's still a good rule to place the vast majority of your scenes in five or six regular locations. Cost remains paramount.

SETTING UP ARENAS OF CONFLICT

The sets will be the places where your characters spend most of their time: sitting rooms, kitchens, offices, pubs. Your choice is based on practicality. Don't try to be too creative. Simply examine their everyday lives. Once you have an idea of what the sets will be, bring them into focus by asking:

- *Where do the characters normally sit/stand?* We drift towards habitual places. In the office, we occupy our designated desk and, in the home, sit on a preferred part of the sofa. In *Cheers*, the regulars at the bar had their own stool. Establishing your characters' typical 'spot' will help you dream up their daily interactions.
- *What do the characters do there?* Look at their habits. Does someone regularly flop down on top of the paper their partner

has been reading? A small action, but it could be the basis of a scene or maybe even trigger an episode.

* *Battleground or meeting place?* Where could the big scenes happen? See your sets as arenas of conflict or places of recuperation. Many sitcoms make use of a café or pub where characters can meet away from the battleground to relax, banter and scheme. In *Friday Night Dinner* the Goodmans' sitting room is a source of embarrassment and opening of wounds as they meet before dinner, but in *Outnumbered* it is somewhere for the Brockmans to regroup after an exhausting day's squabbling.

→ **NOW TRY THIS**

Draw an overall plan of your sitcom location. Lay out each room and how they are joined. This will add an extra dimension and may give you ideas for stories. Do a more detailed plan for each room, the furniture and where each character tends to be found. How do they move about in the room? What are the activities there?

What usually goes wrong with sitcoms . . . people forget about believability. If the show is based on a true situation then let that truth permeate the show. Too many shows (especially of late) have an unbelievable premise or an unbelievable group of characters. Inevitably the audience can't engage with them at all. Writers should ask themselves why anyone would want to watch these people more than once.

Paul Minett and Brian Leveson

Exercise

Where do your characters spend their days and/or nights? Many of the answers will suggest themselves. What kind of building is it and which rooms do they occupy? Is any room associated with a particular character? What kind of rooms are they? Pick five or six rooms or exteriors for your regular sets. In which do your characters work or fight? In which do they relax? Don't try to be over-creative or strive for comedy. Make your sets normal.

EXPRESSING CHARACTER

How can your sets reveal your characters? Del Trotter's flat in *Only Fools and Horses* was full of tasteless tat that he had picked up as a trader. The Goodmans' house in *Friday Night Dinner*, on the other hand, is spotless and bland, expressing Jackie Goodman's home-making style and offering comic possibilities for her messy sons.

WRITING LOCATIONS FOR RADIO

Naturally, this level of detail isn't necessary for radio. You still need, however, to use a limited number of locations. Too many sets will confuse the audience. The BBC's technology will help you set up a large variety of acoustic states (soft carpets, stone floors, echoing chambers, small rooms, etc.) as well as their huge library of sound effects.

When conceiving your radio locations ask:

- *What does this location sound like?* Sound carries differently in a kitchen than an office, for example.
- *How can I establish the location through sound?* Remember how you approached this while writing sketches. A kitchen may involve plates or running water, an office the faint noise of keyboards. Don't overdo this, however.
- *How can I establish the location through the dialogue?* Make this clear without over-explaining. 'Now we're all here in the sitting room' is clunky but 'You're sitting on my end of the sofa' gives the same information and expresses character.

SITCOM TRY-OUT

THE THEME

The sitcom idea I came up with earlier seems to be about frustrated ambition. Cass is desperate to make an artistic impact and despises her everyday job. I see her as having difficulty with the first because her frustrations with the second impede her ability to empathize with people.

THE TRAP

It feels as if Cass stays in the arts centre because there's a flow of people who may help her in her ambitions. It's part of a world in which she longs to play a bigger part. She's been there nearly ten years and is not likely to find another job like this.

THE SETTING

The centre is a crumbling Victorian building in an outer area of London. I'll call it the Old Abattoir Arts Centre. Funding will be a major problem, which could generate some good storylines. Cass will have a messy cramped office dominated by a motivational poster. Self-help books prop up the box files. Gavin and Desi will each have their own office, both bigger than Cass's. Meetings could take place in the canteen, a neutral area with tables made of beer barrels and serving lots of carrot cake.

ESTABLISHING THE CHARACTER'S CONFLICTS

- *Cass and Gavin*: I'm getting to know the characters and have more of a feel for how they get on (or not). Cass has to defer to Gavin, who is frustratingly ten years younger. She is impatient with his jargon and vagueness. He never confronts her. Whenever she asks for more yoga mats, for example, he'll praise her exciting suggestion and do nothing about it. She is in a permanent state of seething with him.

- *Cass and Desi*: Cass regards Desi as an unreconstructed male. She loves to snipe at him but knows she'll get nowhere. Her squabbles with him are frequent but make life more bearable.
- *Cass and Candy*: Candy may be a fellow woman, but she's also conservative, American and believes in angels. She is the one person below Cass in status at the centre, but Cass tries very hard to treat her as an ally, as Candy is far better at dealing with Gavin and Desi than she is. However, she continually bites her lip at Candy's homely views.
- *Cass and Clive*: Clive is like a younger brother. She feels affection for him but can't help pushing him around. She can open herself up to him, knowing he will not be judgemental. But he is not always a willing ally: if she treats him too harshly he will bite back, passive-aggressively or more overtly.

TROUBLESHOOTING

'My characters work in a profession about which I know virtually nothing. How much research do I need to do?'

If you want to write a moderately realistic sitcom, I'm afraid you're going to struggle constructing an episode, let alone a series, if it's on totally alien territory. If you're attempting something more surreal you're freer to create an imaginary world but will still need to give it a strong internal logic with its own detail. If you have some promising characters, try locating them somewhere more familiar to you. Say you have a group of characters who work in the Large Hadron Collider. You'd need a pretty daunting knowledge of science to make that seem real. These characters will be highly intelligent, technical people. Can you locate them somewhere about which you have some knowledge, such as a chemical laboratory or the computer industry?

'The trap that holds my characters together doesn't seem strong enough. I'm worried that they can walk out at any time: there's not enough glue.'

Look closer at your characters. Their emotional needs might give the answer: traps are often non-physical. Think of them as a family, and how there may be hidden or underlying reasons why they stay where they are. Meeting up for dinner once a week, as in *Friday Night Dinner*, doesn't seem much of a trap for a sitcom. But when you realize the importance this regular event has for a Jewish family, you see that none of them is about to break the Friday-night custom any time soon.

SUMMING UP
- Establish the underlying theme of the sitcom and what you are trying to say with it.
- Establish the trap that keeps the characters coming back week after week.
- Decide on the location, making sure it reflects and brings out the characters.
- Decide on your basic sets and how the characters inhabit them.

WRITING SITCOMS: CREATING STORYLINES

All this preparation may make you wonder when you will start to give birth to your baby. Surely the business of a writer is to write: too much planning seems like putting off the proper work. The hours you've been putting in, however, have been essential. Your dialogue will fit the mouths of your characters far better and their actions will keep the wheels of the sitcom rolling rather than flying off.

There's a little bit more groundwork yet to be done. Before embarking on your showcase episode you need to have a rough plan for at least five more. This will give you and the reader much more of a sense of the strength of your sitcom's legs.

THINGS TO CONSIDER WHEN CREATING STORYLINES

MAKE YOUR MAIN CHARACTERS CENTRAL
The actions and decisions (or indecision) of your central cast should carry the plots and build them to their resolution. You may need one-off characters to trigger a story or nudge it forward, but their place is in the back seat as your principals drive things forwards.

CHARACTERS COME BEFORE PLOT
Plot is no more than the actions and words of the characters. When building your plots at all times ask, 'What would they do?' Avoid coincidence and convoluted storylines. Have slapstick moments by all means, but don't let the farce take over.

STAY TRUE TO THE CHARACTERS
If someone acts or speaks out of character the audience will instinctively lose faith in them. Keep your vision of them strong.

Don't alter their essentials unless you've made a clear decision to change the direction of your sitcom.

STAY IN LOCATION
Your characters' reactions and attitude are influenced by their surroundings as much as by each other. If you must move them away from your main sets, think hard about the impact this will have on them and try to keep the balance of the sitcom intact.

THINKING UP EPISODE IDEAS
You can now make good use of all your work on your characters. With a bit of luck, possible storylines will be popping into your head. There are ways of helping the process.

GIVE YOUR CHARACTER A CHALLENGE
I've heard sitcom plots described as thrusting a character up a tree, throwing bricks at them and watching them as they try to climb down. What would test your character? What pressure could bring out their comic flaw? How would they struggle to overcome it?

PRESENT YOUR CHARACTER WITH AN OPPORTUNITY
What do they want? What could happen to make them think they can get it? It could be something trivial or profound.

ASK 'WHAT IF . . .?'
Play around with this question just as you did with sketches. It's like throwing a stone into a pond and seeing the ripples spread, or maybe picking up an object in the hoover and listening to the noise it makes. For example, what would happen to your characters if:

- *A routine is broken?* How would they react to the disruption? How would they cope with the unfamiliar?
- *A long-dreaded event happens?* It could be an everyday worry rather than something catastrophic.

- *An unexpected person arrives?* It could be someone from the past or a stranger who has an impact. You'll need to bring on a non-regular character, which is fine as long as the regulars carry the story.
- *There is a windfall?* What piece of luck could change your character's prospects? How could they be threatened? How would they fight to save them?
- *A subsidiary character makes an unexpected decision?* What impact could this have on other characters?
- *A secret is revealed about one of the characters?* Would it be something shameful, amusing or embarrassing?

→ NOW TRY THIS

In *Friends* the title of every episode began with 'The One with . . .': 'The One with the Cat', 'The One with Ross's Wedding', etc. Try doing this with your sitcom and work out how you could build plots round the titles.

Exercise

Examine three episodes of a well-known sitcom. What is the range of story ideas? Do they all spring from the characters? Do they involve different characters in turn? Now make a list of thirty possible ideas for episodes for your sitcom. Describe them in two or three sentences. Don't think too hard about them or judge them. Focus on how true they are to the characters and situation rather than on how funny they seem.

You have to write badly in order to write well.

William Faulkner

TURNING YOUR IDEAS INTO PLOTS

To evaluate your ideas as possible vehicles for thirty minutes of drama you now need to think critically and analytically.

WHAT WOULD YOUR CHARACTER DO?

How would they react to a triggering event? Would this cause ripples that would spread to the other characters?

HOW COULD THINGS ESCALATE?

Is there a snowball effect? How would your character's emotions change as the story develops? How would this lead them to push the situation further? How could other characters be brought in?

TRIVIAL IS WONDERFUL

You're not writing grand opera or Shakespearean tragedy. Sitcoms can be miniscule. A whole episode of *One Foot in the Grave* was about Victor's increasing paranoia as he looked up symptoms of a minor ailment online. Very little happened – but his powerful fears ignited the comedy.

KEEP TO THE ONE IDEA

Sitcom stories are as tight as sketches. Focus on one incident and its repercussions. A storyline may seem gentle and slow-moving but it will centre round a specific issue and the reactions of the characters. If the story is about a lost hairbrush, stick to the hairbrush and its ramifications. Don't meander.

→ NOW TRY THIS

Imagine a day in your character's life passing entirely normally. This may not sound very dramatic but it could trigger ideas. Ray Galton and Alan Simpson created a classic episode of *Hancock's Half Hour* out of Hancock's boredom during a typical 1950s Sunday afternoon.

USING SUBPLOTS

Subplots can be invaluable in many ways:

- *Keeping the characters occupied*: a subplot keeps more of the cast active. It maintains the audience's interest in characters who don't feature strongly in the main plot. It also keeps the actors busy and happy.
- *Taking the weight off the main plot*: concurrent storylines tend to be simpler with fewer developments than single plots. Building a chain of consequences for each story becomes less involved.
- *Making the sitcom more realistic*: if you use two plots you avoid the temptation to be melodramatic and convoluted. We rarely go through a day chasing just the one objective. A couple of plots varies the focus and feels more normal and everyday.
- *Adding an echo or a counterpoint*: your secondary story can echo the theme of the first or add a revealing contrast. Your paranoid main character could misinterpret the grumpy behaviour of his boss as a sign he is about to get sacked, while at the same time he sees the secret signing of a silver wedding card for him among his colleagues as a whispering campaign.

DECIDING ON WHETHER OR NOT TO USE SUBPLOTS

Do you want to write fuller, overarching plots about one character or keep the balls in the air with a larger group? Do you want to create an everyday effect with a number of cameos or build more overtly dramatic stories? Remember that subplots have been used in single main character sitcoms: *One Foot in the Grave* often had two or even three concurrent storylines about Victor, which exacerbates his paranoia about being picked on by fate.

Don't rush this decision, and listen to your instincts. There are some further considerations with subplots:

- *Staying consistent with the number of plots*: the number of plots in each episode helps determine the rhythm of the series. If you suddenly change from one plotline to two, you alter the feel of the sitcom and can alienate the audience.

- *Dovetailing the subplot with the main story*: the storylines don't have to be entirely separate. The two strands about the paranoid office man above involve him interacting with different people, each shedding light on his character.
- *Using equally weighted plots*: *Friends* became famous for this. No one story predominated; every character was equally important and equally funny.

EVALUATING YOUR EPISODE IDEAS

Once you've considered all the above, you can start to select the most promising episode premises. Go down your list of thirty ideas asking these questions:

- Can this idea be developed into a good story with at least six or seven escalating stages?
- Does this idea centre round your main characters?
- Can your characters move things forward while staying true to themselves?
- Does this idea involve a minimum (two or three at most, ideally only one) of one-off characters for the episode? Do they play only an ancillary role?
- Does this idea entail your characters remaining inside, or at least returning to, their trap?
- Do the characters stay mainly within the usual settings?

BUILDING YOUR PLOTS

Modern filmed sitcoms have a different tone from old-fashioned shows but the fundamental structure stays the same.

THE BEGINNING

- *Introduces the plot trigger*: the events that kick off the story happen in the first scene or two. If you leave it until later you lose dramatic tension and the audience's interest.

- *Foreshadows what the episode is about*: you can use part of the first scene to reveal something about the characters, which will be tested as the episode develops. You can also set up an incident or have someone say something that can be incorporated later on.

- *Reintroduces the audience to the characters*: every week, if you are lucky, a large number of people will watch your sitcom for the first time. Use the first couple of scenes to re-establish your characters, while moving the story forward.

If the audience aren't hooked within the first three minutes, they will reach for their remotes. Your first couple of scenes should be packed full of substance.

THE MIDDLE

- *Escalates the situation*: the action develops step by step until it reaches a climax. The pace may be steady rather than farcical, but the problems and emotions of the characters inexorably deepen. Here are some typical things that can happen:
  - As they try to solve the problem or meet the opportunity, the character meets opposition from another character.
  - The actions of another character, intentionally or unintentionally, become an obstacle.
  - Their own flawed understanding of the situation becomes an obstacle in itself.
  - The character is on their way to solving the problem but a greater problem, arising out of the first one, occurs.
  - Something happens in the subplot that complicates the situation.

- *Builds to a climax*: there is a point of no return at which the characters are forced to confront each other or confront something in themselves. These are typical things that could happen:

- The character is forced to make a decision they had been avoiding.
- Their pretences are finally revealed for all to see.
- At the last minute they turn things round and come out on top.
- The chaos builds until it is completely out of their control.
- It becomes clear that they can't get what they want.

THE END

Sometimes the plot ends abruptly, but it's more usual for the issues to be tied up in an ending that will:

- *Resolve the situation*: the conflict is over until the next episode. Probably, very little has changed but the characters have turned that specific corner.
- *Re-establish the status quo*: in the course of a scene or just a few lines we see the characters back in their usual loop. The trap is still sprung.

→ NOW TRY THIS

Have a go at working backwards. Let images of your characters in a chaotic, pressurized situation drift into your head. Be visual. Make it extreme if you like, as long as it's believable. Imagine this is your climax scene. What did they do to get in the situation? How could the story build to it?

The more serious the subject matter, the funnier it is.

Simon Nye

Exercise

Analyse an episode of a well-known sitcom, either by playing it back or looking at the script. How does the plot develop? How many distinct steps of development are there? How many of the characters are involved? How many scenes does it take to start the plot, how long is the climax scene and is there a scene that re-establishes the status quo? Does the sitcom use subplots?

ANALYSING AN EPISODE OF *THE OFFICE*
(Series One, Episode Two)

- FORESHADOW: In his office, David Brent tries to impress work experience girl Donna with how laidback he is by disregarding voicemail messages and throwing the answering machine in the bin.
- TRIGGER OF PLOT: Brent reassures his staff that they are the most efficient branch of the company and aren't threatened by redundancies.
- FORESHADOW: He introduces Donna to the staff, who make sexist comments.
- FORESHADOW: Gareth and Tim bicker over who will sit next to Donna. Gareth tries to impress her with his mobile phone holster.
- TRIGGER OF SUBPLOT: Brent finds a joke pornographic image of himself on his computer. For Donna's benefit, he makes a show of being offended.
- SUBPLOT: Brent delegates Gareth to grill the staff over who posted the image.
- PLOT: Jennifer from Head Office arrives to quiz Brent over his actions to cut costs and finds he has done nothing. She says he will have to make redundancies.
- SUBPLOT: Tim and Dawn make fun of Gareth's pompous and inept investigation methods.
- PLOT: Brent invents a non-existent person in the warehouse whom he has made redundant. Jennifer makes him show her round.

- SUBPLOT: Gareth makes a mess of interviewing Donna.
- PLOT: Jennifer finds that the redundant person does not exist. She is appalled at the slack and sexist manner of the warehouse personnel.
- SUBPLOT: Tim and Dawn tease Gareth as he quizzes them.
- CLIMAX OF PLOT/SUBPLOT: In front of Jennifer, Brent accuses Tim of posting the image. He is forced to climb down when Tim reveals that the culprit was Brent's friend Finchy.
- RESOLUTION OF PLOT: Brent picks up the phone and makes a show of firing Finchy. Jennifer listens in on the extension: he has been talking to the speaking clock.
- STATUS QUO: We end with Tim revealing his new screensaver: 'Gareth is a Benny'.

The Office eschewed fast-moving farcical plots in favour of a slower, more realistic rhythm, and here there are three short foreshadowing scenes. The main plot, in which Brent tries to cover up his inaction on cost-cutting from Jennifer, runs neatly together with the investigation into the pornographic image. The two storylines merge effectively at the climax. The re-establishment of the status quo, as Tim and Gareth squabble, is done in a very short visual scene.

The episode gets right to the heart of Brent's delusion that his laddish, laissez-faire style makes him a good manager.

Exercise

Pick ten of your thirty ideas which you think are promising. Now narrow them down to six. Using the points we have raised ask yourself which of the six looks the most fruitful. For this one, create the plot and, if you're using one, the subplot. How does the story build to a climax? How is it resolved? Write out the plot step by step.

SITCOM TRY-OUT

I've given the sitcom a title: 'Losing the Plot'.

EPISODE STORYLINE

Uruguayan director Pilar de la Cortesa has been booked to perform her physical theatre play at the Old Abattoir. Cass sees this as a chance to present Pilar with *Andromeda on the Rocks*, a play she's been writing ('It's not a play, it's words with movement'). At a meeting Gavin discusses damp in the dressing room with Desi and persuades Cass to let Pilar use the yoga room for dressing.

Cass tries unsuccessfully to approach Pilar, a haughty diva who thinks Cass is the cleaning lady. Candy suggests to Cass that she gives her a beauty makeover. Cass refuses but Clive agrees to have one. Cass approaches Pilar again just as she discovers cockroaches in the yoga room. She furiously complains, Desi prevaricates and Gavin flannels. Pilar can't believe that the centre is run by such indecisive people and takes the newly smartened Clive to be the director.

Cass interrupts Pilar's meeting with a confused Clive to present *Andromeda* to her. Gavin now insists he's the one in charge. Pilar is furious with Cass who, trying to reingratiate herself, lets her use her office as a dressing room. There she finally manages to present the memory stick containing the play to Pilar. Clive, who has had enough of Cass, makes out to Pilar that she really is the cleaning lady. Baffled and angry, Pilar throws a box file to the floor where she finds, attracted by Cass's old muesli pots, an even bigger nest of cockroaches. She explodes.

TROUBLESHOOTING

'None of my episode ideas seem to build into stories.'

A sitcom plot can seem very slight. It's not like an action movie. What's important is that you get your characters engaged with each other and that there is a bone of contention. If your episode trigger means something to your characters, and you've chosen them well, they will fight over it, however trivial it may seem. Just keep asking, 'What would they do?' Don't force the plot on to them. Let them move it forward.

Don't worry if the plot concept doesn't seem funny at first. If you've drawn good characters, the comedy will emerge. If you still feel your idea doesn't have the heft for a full plot, consider mixing it with a subplot.

SUMMING UP

- Keep your main characters central to the storylines.
- Give them a challenge or an opportunity.
- Stay true to the characters as the story builds.
- Keep to one event for each plotline.
- Use subplots if you have a large number of characters or want a realistic feel.
- Brainstorm thirty plot ideas and narrow them down to ten, then six.
- Give each episode a distinct setup, development, climax and restoration of the status quo.

16
WRITING SITCOMS: BUILDING AN EPISODE

You're very nearly ready to start writing. Before that happy moment, you need to do a final burst of planning.

PLANNING YOUR SCENES

Fine-tune the structure of your episode by dividing it into scenes. Some will carry more weight than others, but look on each one as a building block for your episode.

SCENES HAVE THESE FUNCTIONS:

- To move the action forward.
- To establish where the action takes place, for example, a quick shot of the exterior of the building where the next scene happens.
- To link scenes by showing some action leading up to the next one.
- To act as flashbacks.
- To show concurrent action, maybe as ironic commentary on the main scene or as a quick way to give vital information.
- To add visual variety.
- To vary the pace and rhythm of an episode.

HOW MANY SCENES SHOULD YOU HAVE?

- *TV scripts*: many sitcoms have forty or more scenes. These will often be very short, either flashbacks, establishing shots or cuts. But there will be about ten to thirteen main sequences in which the action moves forward and the characters reveal themselves: these may be interspersed with short scenes.

- *Radio sitcoms*: radio can't do quick scene cuts or visual establishing shots. Too much jumping around between settings confuses the listener. Scenes therefore tend to be longer, with about thirteen to twenty of them.

Exercise

Decide how many scenes you will need. Write out a list that briefly summarizes what happens in each scene.

WRITING YOUR SCENES

Construct your main scenes as you would an episode, with a beginning, middle and end. Try to build the action to a mini-climax, the resolution of which leads to the next scene.

THE BEGINNING

- *Start the scene late*: try jumping to a point after the action has started. For example, if someone has decided to make a crucial phone call, start in the middle of the call with the character reacting to the conversation.

THE MIDDLE

- *Develop the scene in beats*: give your main scenes several steps that carry the story forward. Punctuate these steps with people entering, phone calls, shifts in the conversation, things happening outside and so on. This will add rhythm to the scene.
- *Stay focused on the characters*: what do they want in this scene? What stops them getting it? How do they clash?
- *Be visual*: try to have at least one strong visual moment in each scene.

THE END

- *Get out of the scene quickly*: don't linger. If you can, exit before the action has completed. You will add a lot of pace to the episode.

- *Make the audience anticipate the next scene*: a sense of delicious expectation is the best way to keep their hands off their remote control.

THE SUBPLOT
Splice in the subplot as naturally as you can. Avoid a simple alternating plot–subplot scene order, which creates a predictable rhythm.

> **→ NOW TRY THIS**
> Towards the end of the episode, reincorporate something (a phrase, an action, a prop) that happened earlier. Audiences love it and you will get two laughs rather than one.

If I have one sitcom writing tip to pass on it is this: make sure that there is at least one visual joke in every scene.

Simon Nye

WRITING THE DIALOGUE
The comedy should come from your characters and their reactions rather than jokes. Jokes can be invaluable but they should fit the mouths of the characters who say them, springing naturally out of the situation and not feeling forced. Write the first draft quickly, tuning in to your characters' voices. Build in more laughs in subsequent drafts.

- *Make it natural*: the language should be casual, everyday, twenty-first-century speech, even if you're writing a historically based sitcom.
- *Make it speakable*: this follows from the above. Every time you write a draft, read it out to yourself. Listen out for:

○ Overlong words;
○ Too many adjectives or adverbs;
○ Long rambling sentences;
○ Outdated words;
○ Hard to speak combinations of consonants.

- *Make it economical*: pare the dialogue down to its bare bones. The audience needs less information and fewer words than you think.
- *Keep it in character*: if you hide the character's names in the left-hand column with a ruler, you should still be able to tell who's speaking simply by the voice expressed by the dialogue.
- *Write between the lines*: looks and silences can be more telling than words. Use your characters' reactions. It's fine to have 'THERE IS A BLANK SILENCE' or 'HE CATCHES JENNY'S ANGRY LOOK' in the script. The more we get to know the characters, the more significant their unspoken expressions can be. A good actor can hugely enrich your script with the use of their face. Ask yourself, 'Are there any lines here which could be expressed without words?'
- *Avoid exposition*: lines like 'I've brought you in, Johnny, to discuss this ball in my hand which you kicked into our neighbour Mr Tidy's garden' are undramatic and hard to speak, and annoy the audience.

→ NOW TRY THIS

Interrupt your scene with an extraneous incident at a tense moment: a phone call, someone else enters, someone drops something. How do they react? Can you use this in the dialogue? If you don't use it in the final draft, you'll still have learnt something. If you do use it, this could be an element you could incorporate later.

Exercise

At long last it's now time to write your episode. Have confidence in the work you've done so far and don't worry too much about getting it right. Write your first draft as quickly as you can. The quality of the writing will improve with every draft. Get this one down and you'll be able to correct it later.

REWRITING THE EPISODE

When you've finished it, read it out to yourself. Ask yourself these questions:

CHECK LIST

- Is the episode about thirty minutes long, or twenty-three minutes for ITV, allowing no more than five minutes either way?
- Do the characters drive the plot?
- Do any of the characters need strengthening?
- Can you remove any of the characters without a significant impact on the sitcom?
- Is the concept clear?
- Does the plot move forward a step in each major scene?
- Does the plot have a satisfying climax and resolution?
- Does each scene build?
- Does each scene create anticipation for the next?
- Is the dialogue speakable?
- Does the dialogue express the characters?

You'll notice I didn't add 'Is it funny?' to the list. After weeks of toil, you may well be so familiar with your characters that you find it very hard to answer. Only try to answer that question when you come back to your script refreshed and calm.

Be of good cheer. You've seen your project through: many people would have given up long ago. Give yourself a treat and put your script aside for a week. Now rewrite it. I recommend five rewrites, each time focusing on a different aspect: the characters, the concept, the plot, the scene structure and the dialogue. You'll probably find that your best writing will be done in the rewrites.

Now give yourself another treat!

TROUBLESHOOTING

'My episode's still much too long. I've tried cutting but every scene and character seems indispensable.'

Are you sure there are no unnecessary characters? If one or two of them only exist to supply information or because you think they're hilarious, kill them off. Are two characters very similar? Try amalgamating them. Can you lose a non-regular character? Is your plot too involved? Sitcom storylines only cover a limited distance and are often about minor incidents. Top and tail the scenes further. Go over and over the dialogue several times ruthlessly deleting unnecessary words and phrases. You'll be surprised at how much you can cut.

'After all the rewrites, it's still not funny enough.'

Think about drawing the laughs out rather than putting them in. Visualize your characters' reactions in every scene. Have you ratcheted up the tension enough? The more stress they feel, the funnier they will be. Are you making enough use of any crazies in the cast, without overdoing them?

By this stage you may not be the best judge of how funny your script is. Show it to some professionals, a local writers' group or a reputable script reading service for feedback. Don't show it to your friends – they're not likely to give you useful pointers as to what to do.

And by the way, everything in life is writable about if you have the outgoing guts to do it, and the imagination to improvise. The worst enemy to creativity is self-doubt.

Sylvia Plath

SITCOM TRY-OUT

Here are the first two scenes from 'Losing the Plot', formatted for radio.

CASS'S FLAT. A SOFT MALE VOICE IS TALKING

VOICE:	You can feel the warm sand under your feet as you walk in the ocean. You feel totally relaxed. Hear yourself say it: 'relax'.
CASS:	Relax.
VOICE:	And again.
CASS:	Relax.
FX:	**A DOOR OPENS. CLINKING OF CUPS**
CLIVE:	Hello, Cass. Brought you a cup of tea.
CASS:	Not now, Clive.
VOICE:	Relax.
CLIVE:	Oh, you're doing your hypno programme. I'm sorry.
CASS:	You know I've stopped drinking caffeine.
CLIVE:	Sorry. I'll put it down.
CASS:	Not on the floor.
CLIVE:	It's so you don't have to drink it. Ah, here.
FX:	**SOFT COLLISION**
CLIVE:	Sorry.
CASS:	You've spilt it – all over my bathrobe!
VOICE:	And as the warm ocean water washes over you . . .
CASS:	Clive, you know I hate tea as a drink: I like it even less as a tie-dye.
VOICE:	Never before have you felt so relaxed . . .
FX:	**CLICK. VOICE STOPS**
CASS:	It doesn't work anyway. Imagining I'm on a palm-fringed beach is too much of a stretch. In Catford, anyway.
CLIVE:	Have you tried drinking cocoa?
CASS:	There are plenty of other relaxation techniques. Breathing. Imaging. Locking the door.
CLIVE:	Are you still nervous about meeting Pilar de la Cortesa?
CASS:	She's been my idol for ever. She's the greatest director of physical theatre in . . . in Uruguay anyway. Clive, she's going to love *Andromeda on the Rocks*.
CLIVE:	You've been writing it for four and a half years, Cass. It just has to be good.

CASS:	It's got everything. Iconic mythography. Gender struggle. Seaside setting. When Pilar puts it in her repertoire, I'll be out of Catford and watching the sun set over Ipanema beach.
CLIVE:	I think you'll find that's in Brazil.
CASS:	You've got no imagination, Clive. That's why you're still working in the filing industry. I suppose that's one thing you can do: make tea.
CLIVE:	At least I enjoy it. It stimulates me. Especially when I'm studying my humidity readings. That's where I'm off to.
CASS:	Don't go, Clive! I want you to look at this last scene.
FX:	**KEYBOARDS**
CASS:	I wrote it yesterday. Perseus has just slain the monster and is about to carry Andy off back to Ethiopia. She clocks the situation: dead monster and wet rocks or smug superhero and stifling family. What kind of choice is that for a woman?
CLIVE:	Not much dialogue.
CASS:	It's not a play, Clive. It's movement set to words. Pilar will get it.
CLIVE:	Great! Well, I'm off to check my humidity readings. Last time I looked it was only 28 per cent.
CASS:	Yeah. Roll on Uruguay.
INT:	**GAVIN'S OFFICE. DAY**
GAVIN:	Great, moving on. So, updates on our preparation for the arrival of the Gruppo Teatrico this afternoon. So. The dressing-room wall. Desi?
DESI:	Everything's steady there, Gavin.
GAVIN:	So you mean it's still . . .
DESI:	Yeah, damp.
GAVIN:	Great. Feedback on the silicone treatment?
DESI:	We splashed on a canful. We'll monitor the progress.
GAVIN:	Prognosis for when Pilar de la Cortesa comes into the room?
DESI:	Who knows? But probably – still damp.
CASS:	Gavin, I move that we just move the meeting to the dressing room. Delete our agenda and just prod the wall every quarter hour.
GAVIN:	These daily meetings are important, Cass, so the staff at the Old Abattoir can interface. It's human contact. We're people first, arts administrators second.
	So, Desi, as building manager, your view on the wall.
DESI:	This is an old listed hall, Gavin. Victorian buildings didn't have damp courses. If you ask me, it's part of the charm.

CASS:	Along with the mice.
GAVIN:	Mice? Are they on the agenda?
CASS:	There's not much Desi can do about them. They're listed mice.
DESI:	Cass, if you didn't leave your cheese rolls lying about on your desk . . .
CASS:	Apricot muesli! Cheese rolls are more your style.
GAVIN:	Thanks for your stimulating contribution, Cass. But can we move on to Desi's update on the readiness of the theatre?
CASS:	If Pilar finds a damp patch and mice in the dressing room she's not going to be very receptive.
DESI:	Receptive to what?
CASS:	. . . her inner voice. It's what theatre directors feed on.
DESI:	Can I make a suggestion? If Cass is worried about the mice in the dressing room, maybe she'd be happy for Pilar's artistes to use the studio room?
CASS:	That's where the yoga class is! What about my students?
DESI:	They can swap with the dressing room. All the same to them: they're at one with the universe. They could cope with the mice.
GAVIN:	That's a very exciting suggestion, Desi. Cass?
CASS:	You're asking me to move my yoga learners to a, a . . .
DESI:	Not even to make Pilar de la Cortesa more receptive?
CASS:	. . . OK . . .
GAVIN:	Great!
CASS:	(SIGH) Arts Administrators second – people first.

SUMMING UP

- Structure each scene like a mini-episode with a beginning, middle and end.
- Make each scene move swiftly and don't overuse exposition.
- Make the dialogue flow from the characters rather than deriving it from jokes.
- Reincorporate elements from early in the episode later on.
- Write the episode as quickly as you can and rewrite it several times.

WRITING SITCOMS: MARKETING YOUR SITCOM

Don't worry if your contacts list isn't brimming over with producers and agents. Your main selling point is always going to be your script itself and your belief in it. Adopt a flexible strategy on exposing your work. Writers' groups, script-reading services and online forums can all help you get feedback. Keep a clear head about what you want out of them and you may well find the advice invaluable. Remember that it's your script and you're in control. Be prepared at times for a barrage of sometimes contradictory comments.

Don't send your script out to a producer until you're sure it's as good as you're going to make it. You have one shot with each of them. There's no use sending a reworked script back to someone who's already said 'No'.

WHO TO SEND YOUR SITCOM TO

THE BBC

- *TV*: each BBC television channel has its own style of comedy. With BBC1 it is warm, broad and more geared to families. BBC2 tends to be more left-field and pioneering. BBC3 is younger and edgier while BBC4 sadly no longer produces new material. A good way into BBC3 is through Comedy Feeds (see below).
- *Radio*: BBC Radio 4 has three daily comedy slots. At 11.30 a.m. the sitcoms tend to be more realistic and gentler; 6.30 p.m. is the time for broader humour and sketch shows; and at 11 p.m. the style tends to be more left-field or surreal, often with fifteen-minute episodes.
- *The Script Room*: The Script Room on the BBC website is one of the most important resources for writers. You should refer to it at least

once a week for news on opportunities, layouts, their script library and advice on what the BBC looks for in a new writer. A new writer, by the way, isn't necessarily someone who's young, but a person who has yet to receive a major commission. The Script Room has a twice-yearly window for accepting material, with strict deadlines.

- *Comedy Feeds*: BBC3 runs this online showcase for both sitcom and sketch pilots by emerging comedy talent. It is worth your while looking at the clips on the BBC website.

- *Individual radio producers*: the overworked readers in the Script Room are faced with piles of scripts from hopeful writers. They do recognize and promote talent but to begin with you have no relationship with them. If you target a specific producer, especially on radio, you could find a champion for your work who will open doors for you. Do your homework. When you see or hear a sitcom that has a similar take on the world to yours jot down the name of the producer and send them a carefully worded letter with your attached script. Try to come across as someone with whom they'd love to work. If you haven't heard within a month, follow it up with a phone call. You may get no response or you may begin a relationship that gets your career off the ground. Never send the same script to two producers at the same time, for reasons which should be obvious. Figure 12 gives examples of good and bad emails to producers.

INDEPENDENT PRODUCTION COMPANIES

The BBC gives out a large number of commissions to independent producers for radio and TV. Both large and pocket-sized, established and newly formed, these are the breeding ground for some of the most innovative British comedy. They are often individualistic and freewheeling, and there is no prescribed way to approach them (many of the larger ones such as Baby Cow don't look at new scripts). You'll need to do some homework to find out which ones do comedy and will look at new writers.

From: a.writer@smartplan.com
To: mary.producer@bbc.co.uk

Dear Mary Producer

I've just finished an episode of my radio sitcom 'Jaded'. It's about Jack, an ageing advertising executive who is continually fending off competition from younger, more thrusting colleagues. At the same time he's becoming disillusioned with the world of media and dreams of doing something more 'real', but lacks the courage to make the move.

I'm contacting you because I loved 'The Lower Case' which you produced last year and see 'Jaded' as being in a similar vein, with a naturalistic feel but with heightened characters.

I worked in advertising for four years and 'Jaded' is a passionate project for me. I have had three sketches on 'Newsjack' and write for a sketch group in my home city of Middlewich.

I attach a full episode and synopses of five others, which I hope you enjoy reading.

Many thanks for your time.

- -

From: a.writer@losermail.com
To: mary.producer@bbc.co.uk

Hi Mary

I'm letting you know of a sitcom I've been writing which would fit in to your Thursday evening slot perfectly. However, should you wish to broadcast it in the morning that would be fine by me. It's called 'Jaded', and as the main character is a disillusioned fifty-year-old advertising executive, it would suit the ageing demographic of your channel to a T. I originally designed it as a TV sitcom but have adapted it thoroughly for radio.

I know you must hate having an overcrowded inbox, but I'm sending an entire episode as I'm sure you're going to love it. I feel Peter Capaldi would be perfect as Jack and Janet McTeer would be great as his long-suffering wife Sue.

I feel sure 'Jaded' will go down well as it received a very warm reception at the East Middleshire Writers' Group which I attend. Jenny Chairperson, who ran the meeting, described it as 'having potential'.

I'd be happy to jump on a train at a moment's notice and discuss it with you. I am an easy writer to work with and am always happy to incorporate suggested rewrites. My ambition is to have a sketch show and a sitcom broadcast simultaneously on the BBC, and I genuinely feel that 'Jaded' will help me realize this.

All the best

Figure 12 – Examples of Emails to a Producer

The first shows passion but is professional and succinct; the second is overfamiliar and arrogant, and would probably be deleted along with the unread attachment.

You can find a list of production companies with whom the BBC works on the BBC Writersroom page. Do some research on the excellent *British Comedy Guide* website which lists pretty well every comedy broadcast since time began and includes details on their producers. There is also a directory of the British Film Industry called 'The Knowledge', which lists all independent film-makers.

ITV
ITV sitcoms have traditionally been popular mainstream family comedy, often with a broad style of humour and a warm heart. ITV does not look at unsolicited scripts from writers but receives proposals from production companies (see below), which should be your first port of call.

CHANNEL 4
Channel 4 is the home of edgier, more unconventional comedy. They are looking for non-traditional sitcoms on topics that haven't been tackled before. If your style is more left-field they should be one of your targets. Like ITV they only take sitcoms from production companies. More about them below.

COMEDY BLAPS
This is Channel 4's online comedy showcase. They are looking for new comedy ideas in the form of videos about four minutes long. Ideally the idea should work brilliantly as a short but have the scale and potential to develop further and possibly get a full pilot. They only take submissions from PACT (Producers' Alliance for Cinema and Television) production companies, so get busy researching and contacting independents.

VIMEO
This was set up by a group of film-makers to showcase short films. There are no ads, it's all in HD and there is a strong comedy section.

WHAT TO SEND

THE SCRIPT

The BBC Writers Room now receives submissions via their new e-submissions system. Read the instructions on their web page carefully before sending your material. Your package should include:

- *The finished episode*: this might sound obvious but a lot of hopeful people continue to send in a rough outline and some scribbled character descriptions. A polished and professionally presented complete episode is the only thing that will do. This should be:
  - Word-processed;
  - Formatted correctly;
  - Double-spaced;
  - Page numbered;
  - Fronted with a cover sheet downloadable from the Writersroom page.

  What not to do:
  - Send sketches;
  - Send rewrites of previously rejected material;
  - Send unaccompanied pitches and concepts;
  - Send audio or visual recordings such as DVDs and audio tapes;
  - Send the script simultaneously to elsewhere in the BBC;
  - Use handwriting or exotic fonts;
- *Outlines of future episodes*: on a separate sheet include a 100–200 word synopsis of each of the other episodes. There is no need to double space these or to place each on a separate page.
- *A brief CV – if it helps*: don't neglect to mention any sketches you may have had broadcast or other writing successes. Highlight any specific experience or knowledge of your sitcom setting or characters. Don't bang on about the letter you had in the school magazine or the hilarious person you met on holiday on whom you based your main character. Keep the CV strictly relevant. If you haven't yet had anything broadcast or published, it won't be held against you if you don't include a CV.

- *A covering letter*: this should be brief. If you're contacting a specific director tell them why you're targeting them in two or three sentences.

TO PHONE OR NOT TO PHONE?

Phoning before sending it off is not essential for a warm reception for your script. You may well improve your chances if you make human contact beforehand but be aware that some producers are happier than others to receive unsolicited calls. You're very likely to be talking to a voicemail, in which case don't leave a message but keep trying every couple of hours.

Your voice sounds more confident if you stand up and a smile adds warmth. Always prepare carefully what you want to say. Your introduction could be, 'Hello, my name's . . . I've written "Sinking", a radio sitcom about a fading reality TV star. I loved "Losing Ground" which you produced and feel this is in a similar vein. Would you be interested in having a look at an episode?'

SHOWCASING YOUR SITCOM

Writers' groups across the country regularly meet up for readings, often using professional actors. Hearing a well-performed read-through of your sitcom is a terrific way of seeing what works and what doesn't. Find a group near you, go along to get a feel for how they operate and present your script to them. If you're feeling confident, try inviting some people along from the industry. There is information on writers' groups in the Appendix.

WHERE TO SEND YOUR SCRIPTS

See the list of 'Television Comedy Producers' in the Appendix for a variety of major sitcom producers, including the BBC, ITV and independent companies. Independents range from major companies taking up large tower blocks to tiny outfits working out of someone's kitchen. Always check to see if they receive unsolicited scripts. You may not get past the receptionist one day, but the next you may elicit some useful information.

THE LIFE OF A WRITER

The fact that you've got this far in the book shows you have the determination and staying power to find success as a writer. If you keep researching the markets, making contacts and submitting good material, sooner or later a door will open for you. There will be wonderful highs, but at times you may feel that it would be simpler to mail your submissions back to yourself with 'Rejection' in the subject line. As with anything else worth doing, persistence is key. Staying positive through the difficult times will bring the good times ever closer.

KEEPING GOING WITH YOUR WRITING

MAKE IT FUN

If you stick just one note on to your screen, make it this: 'Make it fun.' You're in the business of giving pleasure to others. It may be hard, challenging work but at all times allow yourself to have a share of the enjoyment you want to give.

ESTABLISH A ROUTINE

Some people are morning writers, others are night owls, others scribble during their lunch break. Find your best time of day to write and incorporate it in your routine, whether it's thirty minutes or three hours. What matters is regularity. You will slowly build up a body of material and you will get to know how long it will take you to produce a number of pages. You're a writer. Make it a central part of your daily life.

SET GOALS AND STICK TO THEM

Every week, plan what you aim to achieve, whether it's two sketches or ten pages of your sitcom. Stick to the goals through thick and thin. If you find that you are regularly missing the goal, reduce it to a more realistic level. Always factor in time to research new markets and outlets.

BE PROACTIVE
Don't wait for the work to come to you. Create your own opportunities. Get to know actors, directors, film makers and friendly publicans (you see, it's not all painful). Research the internet, stage a show, join a writers' group. Everywhere you go, at work, in the pub, over coffee, let people know you're a comedy writer.

WATCH A LOT OF COMEDY
Keep up with the latest sitcoms and sketch shows on TV and radio, but also reacquaint yourself with the classics. Become a regular at your local standup comedy club.

DON'T GIVE UP
Writers of hit TV series don't wake up one morning and, out of the blue, come up with a great idea. Before that, they'll have worked for years on failed projects, written uncommissioned sitcoms and watched rejections pile up. Doing this they will have accumulated the experience and cussedness that helped to bring their success. Writing is a long game.

You don't put your life into your writing. You find it there.

Alan Bennett

HANDLING REJECTION
Rejection is as much part and parcel of a writer's life as dust in the air. Understanding that will help you deal with it. There are many reasons why scripts are not accepted, many of which are not to do

with the quality of the work. There are various types of rejection, each of which mean subtly different things.

ENCOURAGING REJECTIONS

If you get any kind of feedback, your submission, even though rejected, may have gone down well. If the reader or producer has taken the trouble to make a specific response, it's a sign they see something in your work. Think about the feedback, take it on board if it makes sense, make a note of the producer and make them a target for your next project

DISCOURAGING REJECTIONS

These usually take the form of a curt pro forma 'Not for us' or 'We can't see a way of producing your script at this time.' It's a pretty definite 'no' but don't be too disheartened. Perhaps they already have a sketch on a similar topic, a sitcom with a similar format in pre-production or the similar show is being discontinued. Don't cross the company or producer off your list until you're convinced that they really are wrong for you.

NO RESPONSE

Unfortunately this happens a good deal. Don't get upset. If the show has advertised that they are looking for non-commissioned writers, they will be too busy to reply. Maybe the producer was working a twelve-hour day on another project and couldn't give you the time. Perhaps the company are not accepting submissions. Check their website before sending anything else off to them.

The only writers who don't get rejections are the dreamers who never submit. Tell yourself that each turn-down brings you closer to the inevitable success. The best bulwark against diminished confidence is to keep on writing. Your next sketch, sitcom or series of jokes is more important than the silence that perhaps greeted your last batch. Maybe this will be the one that leads to that nice email and payment. Sooner or later, it will.

WHY SCRIPTS ARE REJECTED

In my experience of producing stage sketch shows, my partner and I found that half the submissions were completely unusable. The writers had clearly not read the guidelines. There were un-reformatted extracts from TV sitcoms and non-topical humour for a satirical show. Many of the sketches were old material only cursorily reworked or not reworked at all. Another 20 per cent only followed the guidelines vaguely, while a further 20 per cent fitted the brief but weren't very funny.

This left the final 10 per cent of sketches that were both funny and apposite, and over which we argued for hours. We reluctantly had to turn down some good material because other sketches fitted the show better.

By working on your craft, properly reading the guidelines and being punctilious with your submissions, make it your aim to join that 10 per cent of writers. You have control over that.

WRITING WITH A PARTNER

Galton and Simpson, Clement and La Frenais, Andy Hamilton and Guy Jenkin – some of the greatest comedy has been written by duos or even trios and quartets. Most comedy writers consider joining up with someone else at some stage in their career.

THE ADVANTAGES OF WRITING WITH A PARTNER

- *You can gauge how funny your writing is*: you have someone to give instant feedback and you will agonize less over whether an idea or a line will get a laugh.
- *You can create a wider range of ideas*: two minds are better than one. You will be able to brainstorm twice the number of concepts for jokes, sketches and sitcoms.
- *You feel more secure*: you will have pored over and discussed every script you send out. You know that at least one other person

thinks it works. You are more able to face criticism and rejection – it feels less personal.

- *You break the isolation*: a good writing partnership is more like a marriage than a business arrangement. You can share your hopes and worries, and of course have a laugh together.

THE DISADVANTAGES OF WRITING WITH A PARTNER

- *You need to compromise*: at times you will feel that your unique voice is being stifled for the sake of the partnership. You may have to cut or amend what you feel are your best ideas if the other person isn't keen on them.
- *You need to share the vision*: it's possible to work with someone for some time before realizing that the two of you see the project very differently. There'll have been false starts, arguments, slow progress or maybe just a sloppy script and a lot of pain.

Spend at least 15 minutes a week in front of the mirror alone doing nothing but affirming yourself and convincing yourself that you have a voice and it is a damn funny voice. When the world then tells you your writing sucks, well you at least have some self-belief to cope with rejection.

Brent Quinn

PRESENTING YOURSELF AS A COMEDY WRITER

The great thing about being a writer is that no one expects you to wear a suit or behave formally or deferentially. Some looseness in appearance and behaviour is accepted among creative people. But only a certain amount. You need to come across as professional: your personal reputation is as important as your reputation as a writer.

I will never forget a showcase in which scenes from new sitcoms were performed before some well-known TV producers. One of the writers became very drunk and started to denigrate all the other scripts, before loudly complaining that everyone was too old. Needless to say, she wasn't given a commission.

Carry yourself proudly as a writer. You've followed a path that most people would find too challenging. Value your trade and your ability. This also means valuing other writers and supporting them, being readier to pass on information and encouragement than unsolicited criticism.

DO:

- Make use of meetings and networking for news of opportunities.
- Have a card that you carry with you always.
- Put aside modesty and let the world know of your successes.

DON'T:

- Denigrate successful writers and producers.
- Show bitterness or too much self-deprecation about any perceived failure of your own.
- Try to be funny all the time. Present yourself as a normal, listening, person.

SUPPORT AND DEVELOPMENT

WRITERS' GROUPS
These are invaluable not only in hearing your script assessed, but in overcoming isolation, for networking and simply for getting out of an evening.

COMEDY WRITING COURSES
These can be very useful as long as you are clear about what you want to get out of the course and don't expect the teacher to solve all your writing problems. If you adopt a positive attitude you stand

to learn something new and valuable, meet other writers, and revive your energy and focus.

SCRIPT-READING SERVICES

Reading and critiquing a script properly is time-consuming, so a good service won't necessarily be cheap. A useful critique will point out where work is needed and judge your script by what you are trying to achieve: a bad one may leave you either deflated or over-optimistic about it. Check the credentials of the reader or listen to word of mouth.

ONLINE WRITERS' FORUMS

These can be great for gossip, online networking, news and the occasional opportunity.

APPENDIX:
USEFUL RESOURCES
AND ORGANIZATIONS

WEBSITES

BBC (www.bbc.co.uk/writersroom):
  This should be a regular port of call; a mine of information about what's
  happening, advice, script formatting, etc.

Channel 4 Commissioning (www.channel4.com/info/commissioning)
  Receives ideas and proposals from production companies.

Comedy Blaps (http://comedyblaps.channel4.com)
  Receives ideas and proposals from both production companies and individuals.

Comedy Feeds (www.bbc.co.uk/programmes/p01bhx0w):
  BBC3's online showcase for filmed new comedy.

E4 (www.e4.com)
  Channel 4's online presence.

British Comedy Guide (www.comedy.co.uk):
  An excellent and encyclopaedic site, with extensive information for writers on
  opportunities, courses and advice.

Chortle (www.chortle.co.uk):
  The UK guide to comedy gigs also has a busy writers' forum.

Dave's Comedy Festival (www.comedy-festival.co.uk):
  This major festival in Leicester runs a prestigious writers' competition.

Newsjack (https://twitter.com/NewsjackBBC):
  The twitter page for BBC's main outlet for new sketch writers.

Writers' Digest (www.writersdigest.com):
  An American site dealing in all genres of writing.

John Vorhaus (http://radarenterprizes.com):
  Excellent advice for comedy writers from American comedy guru.

Tony Kirwood (www.tonykirwood.co.uk):
  The author's website with tips and information on all genres of comedy writing
  and details of courses.

Shooting People (https://shootingpeople.org):
  Network of film creatives.

Vimeo (http://vimeo.com):
  Online showcase for film and video work.
NewsBiscuit (www.newsbiscuit.com):
  Satire website.
DeadBrain (www.deadbrain.co.uk):
  Satire website.
About.com Animation (http://animation.about.com/od/recommendedreading/a/
  getting-started-in-animation-from-the-comfort-of-your-home.htm):
  Tips from About.com for new animators.
Adobe Flash Professional (www.adobe.com/uk/products/flash.html):
  Animation software.
Freesound (http://freesound.org):
  Database of copyright-free sounds for animation and filming.
Casting Call Pro (www.castingcallpro.com):
  Actors' and casting website.

TELEVISION COMEDY PRODUCERS

Contact addresses for some major national television and independent sitcom and sketch-show production companies:

BBC Writersroom (www.bbc.co.uk/writersroom)
4th Floor, BBC Grafton House, 371–381 Euston Road, London NW1 3AU
Tel: 0208 743 8000

BBC Radio Comedy (www.bbc.co.uk/radio)
BBC Broadcasting House, London W1A 1AA
Tel: 020 7580 4468

BBC Scotland (www.bbc.co.uk/Scotland)
40 Pacific Quay, Glasgow G51 1DA
Tel: 0141 422 6000

BBC Wales (www.bbc.co.uk/wales)
Broadcasting House, Llandaff, Cardiff CF5 2YQ
Tel: 029 2032 2000

ITV Network Ltd (www.itv.com)
200 Grays Inn Road, London WC1X 8XZ
Tel: 020 7156 6000

Scottish Television (STV) (www.stv.tv)
Pacific Quay, Glasgow G51 1PQ
Tel: 0141 300 3000

The Comedy Unit (www.comedyunit.co.uk)
Glasgow TV and Film Studio, Unit D, Glasgow North Trading Estate, 24
Craigmont Street, Glasgow G20 9BT
Tel: 0141 305 6666

Baby Cow Productions (www.babycow.co.uk)
33 Foley Street, London W1W 7TL
Tel: 010 7612 3370
Room 84, The Greenhouse, Broadway, Salford Quays M50 2EQ
Tel: 0161 7133 656

Hat Trick Productions (www.hattrick.co.uk)
33 Oval Road, London NW1 7EA
Tel: 020 7184 7777

Hartswood Films Ltd (www.hartswoodfilms.co.uk)
3a Paradise Road, Richmond, Surrey TW9 1RX
Tel: 020 3668 3060

Objective Productions Ltd (www.objectiveproductions.com)
3rd Floor, Riverside Buildings, County Hall, Westminster Bridge Road,
London SE1 7PB
Objective Scotland, Film City Glasgow, 4 Summertown Road,
Glasgow G51 2LY
Tel: 020 7202 2300

Retort (www.retort.tv)
20–21 Newman Street, London W1T 1PG
Tel: 020 7861 8000

Sideline Productions (www.sideline.ie)
9 Appian Way, Dublin 6, Ireland
Tel: +353 1 631 5310

Talkback Productions (www.fremantlemediauk.com)
20–21 Newman Street, London W1T 1PG
Tel: 020 7861 8000

Tiger Aspect Productions (www.tigeraspect.co.uk)
4th Floor, Shepherd's Building Central, Charecroft Way, London W14 0EE
Tel: 020 7434 6700

WRITERS' GROUPS

London Comedy Writers (www.londoncomedywriters.com):
  A group of writers and actors who meet up fortnightly to read scripts. Sketch
  showcases are performed at intervals. Their website contains news,
  competitions and articles.
Player-Playwrights (www.playerplaywrights.co.uk):
  London's longest-established writers' group with some prestigious comedy
  names amongst its alumni. Weekly readings of all kinds of scripts and
  performances of showcases.
Writers Online (www.writers-online.co.uk/Writers-Groups/Category/Scriptwriter):
  This website includes a directory of UK writers' groups, including scriptwriters'
  circles.

OTHER ORGANIZATIONS

London Sketchfest (www.londonsketchfest.com):
  Festival and showcase for British sketch comedy.
The Sitcom Mission (www.comedy.co.uk/sitcom_mission):
  A competition for new sitcoms that are judged by major figures in the industry.
  Performances are in London but the writers come from across the UK.
The Sitcom Trials (www.sitcomtrials.co.uk):
  Competitions for new sitcoms held in Bristol, Manchester and London;
  attracts industry names and future major talent.
Salford Sitcom Showcase (www.bbc.co.uk/mediacentre/latestnews/2012/sitcom-
  showcase.html):
  Northern-based BBC showcase, which has led to major sitcom commissions.
Funny Women (www.funnywomen.com):
  Helping women to perform, write and do business with humour; runs
  competitions for female standup comedians and comedy writers.
The Writers' Guild of Great Britain (www.writersguild.org.uk):
  The trade union for British writers.
The Society of Authors (www.societyofauthors.net):
  Protects the rights of authors.

British Society of Comedy Writers (www.bscw.co.uk)
  The BSCW provides seminars, networking opportunities and information for
  UK comedy writers.
Greeting Card Association (www.greetingcard.org):
  Includes information, resources and tips for writers of greetings cards.
Spotlight (www.spotlight.com):
  The UK's foremost actors' directory.

PUBLICATIONS

Newspapers and Magazines
Broadcast (www.broadcastnow.co.uk):
  Weekly magazine giving information on production companies.
The Stage (www.thestage.co.uk):
  Weekly newspaper for the arts.

Scripts
BBC Books (www.bbcshop.com):
  Stocks many books of sketch and sitcom scripts.
Channel 4 Books (www.randomhouse.co.uk):
  Produces some sitcom scripts.
Penguin Books (www.penguin.co.uk):
  Produces some TV scripts.

Books on writing
How to Write Comedy by Brad Ashton, Elm Tree Books, 1983.
Writing Comedy by John Byrne, A & C Black, 2004.
Writing Sitcoms by John Byrne and Marcus Powell, A & C Black, 2003.
The Serious Guide to Joke Writing by Sally Holloway, Bookshaker, 2010.
Comedy Writing Step by Step by Gene Perret, Samuel French, 1990.
Comedy Writing by Jenny Roche, Teach Yourself Books, 1999.
The Comic Toolbox by John Vorhaus, Silman-James Press, 1994.
Writing Comedy by Ronald Wolfe, Robert Hale, 2003.
Successful Sitcom Writing by Jurgen Wolff, St Martin's Press, 1996.

Books on comedy
Now That's Funny! by David Bradbury and Joe McGrath, Methuen, 1998.
The Naked Jape by Jimmy Carr and Lucy Reeve, Penguin, 2007.
Classic Radio Comedy by Mat Coward, Pocketessentials, 2003.

Directories

Writers' & Artists' Yearbook, Bloomsbury, 2014:
UK guide to the book, magazine, TV and radio industries.

Contacts by Kate Poynton, Spotlight, 2014 (www.contactshandbook.com):
Directory of the UK TV, stage, radio and film industry aimed at actors, but of general use.
The Knowledge (www.theknowledgeonline.com):
Directory of the UK film and TV production industry.
Westminster Reference Library (www.westminster.gov.uk/services/libraries):
The foremost library for the performing arts in London.

COURSES

Going on a creative writing course can stimulate you, put you in touch with other writers and give you insights into the industry. Across the UK there are full-length courses, weekend and day seminars, and email distance courses. If you're thinking of an email course, check the credentials of the tutor and try to ring them for a chat to see if it's for you. Find out as much as you can about the course and the tutor, especially whether they have had experience in the industry and are not simply academics. The following provide comedy writing courses:

Richmond Adult Community College (www.racc.ac.uk)
City Lit (www.citylit.ac.uk)
Comedy Courses by the Sea (www.comedycourses.biz)
Jan Etherington's Comedy Writing Course (www.comedycourse.biz

ACKNOWLEDGEMENTS

Thanks to: Peter Vincent, Paul Minett and Brian Leveson, Brent Quinn, Alan Stafford, Lynne Parker, Dave Baker, Richard Woolford, Jack Sheppard, Peter Bradwell and Ffion Jones. For their script advice over the years, everyone at Player-Playwrights and the London Comedy Writers. To Ken Rock and the British Society of Comedy Writers. To all my students. And to my wife Mervion for her patience and support.

INDEX